How to Pray

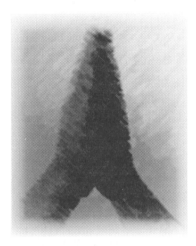

Joseph Nassal, C.P.P.S.
and Nancy Burke

Produced by
The Philip Lief Group, Inc.

Health Communications, Inc.
Deerfield Beach, Florida

www.hci-online.com

Library of Congress Cataloging–in–Publication Data

Nassal, Joe
  How to Pray/Joseph Nassal and Nancy Burke.
      p. c.m.
    "Produced by the Philip Lief Group, Inc."
    Includes bibliographical references.
    ISBN 1-55874-635-8
    1. Prayer I. Burke, Nancy.   II. Philip Lief Group.   III. Title
BL560.N37   1998
291.4'3–dc21
                                                98-40413
                                                CIP

Publisher: Health Communications, Inc.
              3201 S.W. 15th Street
              Deerfield Beach, Florida 33442-8190

Cover design by Sandy Brandvold.

*More things are wrought by prayer
than this world dreams of.*

ALFRED, LORD TENNYSON

Contents

Introduction

WHOM OR WHAT DO WE PRAY TO?

Know first, the heaven, the earth, the main,
The moon's pale orb, the starry train,
Are nourished by a soul,
A bright intelligence, whose flame
Glows in each member of the frame. . . .

VIRGIL

There is a God within us.

OVID

T here is an oft-told modern tale that I first read in Sophy Burnham's lovely book, *Angel Letters*, where it was attributed to Gil Gross of WOR-Radio in New York City. But I have heard and seen variations of the same story elsewhere.

As the "true" story goes, a young couple brought home their new infant son to meet his four-year-old sister. The baby had been home only a few hours when his sister began to insist that she needed to be alone with him. The parents, suspecting sibling rivalry and fearing that the girl might unintentionally hurt the baby, at first refused her request and wouldn't leave her alone with the infant. But the young girl was adamant about needing to spend some time with her baby brother. When her parents asked her why this was so important, she said she couldn't tell them. She just needed to see her brother alone.

Finally, the little girl was so tearfully insistent that she wore down her parents' resistance, and early one evening (after placing an infant monitor in the baby's crib), they allowed the little girl to visit the baby alone. As soon as her parents left the room, the little girl leaned into the crib and began whispering to her brother. In the living room, over the infant monitor, her parents heard this plaintive plea:

"Quick," the young girl said to her baby brother. "Tell me about God. I'm beginning to forget."

*The soul is the sense of something higher
than ourselves . . . a burning desire to breathe
in this world of light and never to lose it—to
remain children of light.*

ALBERT SCHWEITZER

Beginnings: Reclaiming Our Divinity

It has been said by some theologians and spiritual writers—attempting to explain the ever-growing interest in matters Divine—that our dilemma is not so much that we are human beings struggling to be spiritual, but that we are and always have been spiritual creatures grappling with the trappings of our humanity, our wings clipped, our feet fettered to an alien world. I believe that to be true, and I believe the story just shared, apocryphal or not, poignantly illustrates that truth.

We are, in fact, gloriously wrought vessels who come into this world filled to the brim with God. But time and the ebb and flow of human matters both marvelous and mundane drain the light-filled waters at our core. The infant in the story, still close to the source of the heavenly stream, radiates his Divinity. He is a child of light. His sister recognizes this right away. His parents may sense it, but they don't understand it and couldn't put a name to it; they have wandered too far from the source, weary from jumping the hurdles of education, career, marriage, money, mortgage, parenthood. They are dry at their centers.

The young girl, however, is still close to the source and remembers its warm glow. Sadly, she sees that she may be losing what her brother has in abundance, what is also her rightful heritage—to be one of the "children of light." And so she throws up to heaven perhaps the first prayer of her young life, saying in effect, "Talk to me, God. Talk to me. I'm beginning to forget You! Have You forgotten me?"

God is an unutterable sigh in the human heart.

HAVELOCK ELLIS

God and the Impulse to Pray

We can glean much more from this story, especially if we are just beginning the extraordinary journey of prayer and are looking for inspiration and wisdom to buoy our prayerful impulses.

There is the easy nearness of children to God, thanks to their lack of fear of and absolute faith in someone who is at once both greater than and part of themselves. This is something we can learn to emulate as we approach the Divine in prayer.

There is the ability to recognize God in ourselves and in others. It is an awareness that at first feels like a shared secret between kindred spirits. Prayer enlarges our awareness of the Divinity in everyone and everything around us.

There is the intimation that who and what we are at our core is ultimately mystery, and so we search for great answers, marvelous truths, a deeper understanding of who we are and what we are meant to be and do. Prayer is the doorway to that deeper understanding, to an ultimate truth.

Soon, if we hold our hearts open wide, we come to learn that something precious within us may have been lost—perhaps just a piece of the Divine—and we yearn to reclaim it. Prayer is our act of reclamation.

All of these feelings, yearnings, intimations, and searching for answers and truths are among the myriad impulses that drive our desire to pray, that feed our hunger to return to the wellspring of our being, that propel us into the embrace of the Divine.

Finding a God to Pray To

But into whose arms do we leap? From whom do we seek comfort and understanding, receive love and compassion? To whom or to what do we pray? Before we can even begin the journey of prayer, we need a focus, an image, an idea, a destination.

Sadly, this is a major spiritual stumbling block for many people who have been raised on forbidding and punitive gods, unrelentingly male gods, cartoon-like gods, indifferent gods, mute gods, deaf gods, or simply no gods at all. For these people, the "face of God" may be alternately frightening, repulsive, inaccessible, laughable or unimaginable. How can we pray to that which is fearful, unrecognizable or simply not believable?

The answer is that we often must re-envision God for ourselves—create an image of the Divine that strikes a uniquely personal and deep chord that has a special meaning to each of us. We can start the process of re-envisioning the Divine by looking at and perhaps discarding some of the stereotypical notions of God that no longer work for us.

I am the Alpha and the Omega,
the beginning and the ending. . . .

REVELATIONS 1:8

The God of Our Childhood:
A Janus–Faced Divinity?

Many of us raised in Western religious traditions both Christian and Jewish, and in some Eastern ones as well, were taught a narrow and limiting vision of God. He was invariably male and maddeningly two–faced. On the one hand, He could be a benevolent grandfather–type figure: the elderly, radiant, wise and loving God of flowing robes and beard who lived among the clouds and especially cherished children. On the other hand, God could also be a relentlessly punitive judge and taskmaster: the dark and angry God who kept track of each of our sins and failings, exacted punishment, expected penance, threatened banishment, and brought down catastrophes upon our heads in retribution.

Since we were also invariably taught to call this two–faced God our "Father," a word charged with such deeply personal feeling and meaning, many of us were at first confused, if not downright frightened by, the presence of such a duplicitous Divinity in our midst. Later, we often turned away from both versions of this Janus–faced God, the fairy tale grandfather and the cop. But it was hard, if not impossible, to turn away from God as Father. "He" was everywhere, in everything we read, everything we heard, everything we saw.

*Our Father, Who art in Heaven
Hallowed be Thy name. . . .*

THE LORD'S PRAYER

*As truly as God is our Father, so
truly is God our Mother. . . .*

JULIAN OF NORWICH

God as Father, God as Mother

Perhaps no issue in contemporary spirituality and religion has been more galvanizing—and polarizing—than that of God and gender. Whole books have been written about reclaiming the feminine face of God, and most have as a central theme the repudiation of God as some universal father-figure.

Young children and older people from conservative religious backgrounds—and almost every television evangelist—appear to accept with grace and ease the long-held habit of calling the Divine "Father" and only "Father." Others, among them many women and not a few men, including priests, rabbis, monks and ministers, find the idea of an exclusively male deity limiting to their spiritual growth, if not downright offensive.

The tradition began long ago, and it was partly a cultural phenomenon and certainly a political one. But we also contributed to the confusion ourselves, when we decided to reinvent the Divine in our own image.

Humanizing God

Of course, anthropomorphizing God—that is, giving human characteristics to something that is ineffable—should be a moot point. We cannot possibly have any real conception of what form God takes. God is God.

But we are human, and we wanted "someone" to pray to. We also have finite frames of reference, especially for things spiritual and evanescent. So we made the Divine part of our finite world and reframed God in the familiar forms, faces, objects and feelings that we live with. We made God like us, and in many ways, this has served us quite well.

Oh senseless man, who cannot possibly make a worm and yet will make Gods by the dozens!

MICHEL DE MONTAIGNE

Gods and Goddesses

The ancient Greeks and Romans formalized the practice of humanizing the Divine, giving us a cavalcade of magnificent and varied gods and goddesses who were also achingly vulnerable to human failings and temptations.

The Greeks and Romans were just following a long tradition established by even older, nature-based religions throughout the ancient world that always viewed the Divine as both male and female. And these male and female gods were not stereotypical constructs. Female gods could be strong and vulnerable, compassionate and warlike, drawn to the hearth and drawn to the hunt. Male gods, too, encompassed characteristics of both genders, and ran the gamut from the sublime to the ridiculous, the ferocious to the tender. Some even gave birth to half-human and half-divine creatures.

Even early translations of the Old Testament contained references to God in Genesis as *Elohim*, a Hebrew word that refers to the Divine in the plural and connotes both the male and female gender.

When the Gods were more manlike,
Men were more godlike.

JOHANN FRIEDRICH VON SCHILLER

The Loss of the Feminine Divine

Women began to lose their Divinity as Judaism and Christianity became more formalized and widespread. It happened fast and it happened arbitrarily; and we are still feeling the reverberations of this radically masculine shift in the Divine today.

Nature-based religions continued to flourish along with their male and female gods, but they soon became overshadowed, if not eradicated, by the Judeo-Christian movements. Those small bands of worshipers that did survive were labeled "pagans" (*pagani*, or "country-dwellers") by the Romans, because they maintained their rituals and worshiped their gods and goddesses secretly, in obscure and out-of-the-way forest enclaves. They became the forerunners of those who worship the Divine in nature today and who celebrate Earth goddesses.

Other great religions of the same period, Hinduism and Buddhism, to name just two, still revered the feminine in the Divine, though they would later accord mortal women the same second-class status the Western religions would. Nevertheless, the Hindu feminine God, Shakti, also known as Devi, is considered the driving elemental force that sustains the universe. She is one manifestation among many in the Hindu religion of the feminine face of God.

In Buddhism, which is essentially a nontheistic "religion," the great Buddhist saint of compassion, the revered Kuan-yin, has had goddess status since the tenth century. And female Buddhist monks have always worshiped alongside male monks, though for centuries they were not allowed to lead congregations. Among Tibetan Buddhists, the Dakini are profound manifestations of the Feminine Divine, goddesses of universal and primordial wisdom, similar to the Hebrew feminine manifestation of God, Sophia—or Hokhmah—and the feminine God, Shekhinah, from the Kabbalistic tradition of Judaism.

Hinduism and Buddhism, however, despite pre-dating Christianity and having many followers, would never have the reach and power of the Western religions, and their reverence for the Feminine Divine would remain almost exclusively a phenomenon of the East.

In the West, on the other hand, the Judeo-Christian view of religion as patriarchal both in origin and in lineage—and eventually in practice—took hold like wildfire in civilizations and cultures dominated by men. These religions revered a male God, venerated male prophets, ordained male priests and rabbis, and recruited male disciples. Women were asked to step to the back, cover their heads, keep themselves clean and run a good home.

Sophia and Shekhinah all but disappeared from the everyday lexicon of Judaism. And Mary—the young

Jewish girl who gave birth to the Christian God-Man, Jesus, who would radicalize the relationship between humanity and God—was respected less for her inextricable connection to the Divine and more for her humble compliance about being God's willing and unwitting vessel. In all of the New Testament she says barely two dozen words, and most of them are reiterations of Old Testament verse.

The repercussions for women of this great shift to a solely masculine God were enormous. In worship, in liturgy, in religious literature, women lost their voice, their selfhood, their potency, their spiritual integrity. Not only were they excluded from serving as priests, rabbis and ministers; they weren't even allowed to serve at the altar until just thirty years ago. To add insult to injury, most priests, rabbis and ministers were held to vows of celibacy and enjoined to avoid ordinary female companionship.

When it came to prayer, amazingly, women were still expected to revere and worship a masculine God who seemed to be sending a message through His priests and rabbis that women were intrinsically inferior and unworthy of communion with the Divine—unless, of course, they were sanctified mothers or celibate nuns.

That women maintained deep relationships with the Divine, despite their second-class status, and passed this capacity along to their children, is alone a testament to the consummate Godhood in their natures. Women were also, of course, always looking for alternative spiritual avenues, sometimes on the sly, and quietly gathering up and saving the pieces of their discarded Divinity for a better day.

Reclaiming the Feminine Face of God

Though it may seem that it is only in the last twenty-five years or so that women have been fighting to reclaim the feminine face of God in Western religion, the truth is that there is a long modern history, at least as old as Christianity, of celebrating the feminine aspects of God.

The Gnostic Christians, who flourished for several centuries after the birth of Christ—and at the same time as the exclusionary Christian groups who persist to this day—always believed in a Divine Mother, a "Mother of the All" who was the embodiment of wisdom and who coexisted equally with a Divine Father. Indeed, they took the Feminine Divine a step further and called Her the "Holy Spirit," making Her the third Divinity of the Christian Holy Trinity, which includes God the Father and His son, Jesus.

Needless to say, the Gnostic Christians were condemned as heretics by fundamentalist Christians, who preferred their deities purely male.

Nevertheless, the greatly revered English Christian mystic, Julian of Norwich, took up this same Gnostic theme in the fourteenth century. She, too, envisioned the feminine aspect of God as both Divine Mother and as embodied Wisdom. Like the Gnostics, Julian placed her Divine Mother squarely within the Trinity. "God almighty is our loving Father," she said, "and God all wisdom is our loving Mother, with the love and the goodness of the Holy Spirit, which is all one God, one Lord."

*In God we live and move and have
our being.*

ST. PAUL

Jesus as Spiritual Mother

Julian then took a giant leap forward in her envisioning of the Divine Mother and named Jesus as our "true Mother." She justified this by reminding us that Jesus' radical offering of a new kind of spirituality, one that emphasized classically "feminine" attributes such as love, forgiveness, compassion and service to others, began in a woman's womb and was in itself a powerful act of procreation. Just as an earthly mother bodily brings us into the world, Jesus, our spiritual Mother, was driven to spiritually birth us into a new life, a new way of believing and behaving. And just as a biological mother "gives her child to suck of milk," Julian says, "our precious Mother Jesus feeds us with Himself in the Blessed Sacrament."

This was radical stuff for 1393, especially coming from a cloistered noblewoman who lived in spiritual and literal solitude all her adult life. But Julian's words and revelations have endured through the centuries—and are especially popular and relevant today—because they are a deeply intelligent, rational and heartfelt attempt to reconcile the feminine and masculine aspects of God, and bring healing and wholeness to the relationship between humanity and the Divine, the Church and its people.

[God is] . . . a sense sublime
Of something far more deeply interfused,
Whose dwelling is the light of setting suns,
And the round ocean and the living air,
And the blue sky, and in the mind of man.

WILLIAM WORDSWORTH

God as Spirit

As contemporary Catholics we are heartened by Julian's revelations and the renewed attention they are receiving. Her visions of a feminine aspect in the Divine Trinity and of Jesus as our Spiritual Mother hold much resonance and meaning for us, as we meet with diverse groups of people who are looking for new ways to envision the Divine. We see in Julian's re-imaging of God the potential for healing and unity, and for a more inclusive Divinity that embraces and venerates equally all aspects of humanity.

As Christians, we also believe in the mystery of a triad God, a threefold Divinity embodied in the Trinity as God the Father, Christ the Son and the Holy Spirit. And we are comfortable envisioning that Spirit as imageless and all-encompassing, a genderless Divinity that bypasses the boundaries of sex and religion, culture and politics.

For us, Spirit is also the mysterious wellspring from which wisdom, beauty, joy, peace and grace spontaneously rise: unmerited gifts, like a rush of cool, sweet-scented wind on a hot, dry day. A fitting image, for the word "spirit" has its roots in the Latin *spiritus* and *spirare*, meaning "breath," "spirit" and to "breathe" or "blow."

In fact, in some translations of Genesis, God fashions the first human from a lump of mud and blows Divine Breath into the human's nostrils to bring it to life. This is a potent image of how we are simultaneously and eternally body and Spirit, organically connected to the Divine.

In our lives we try to follow the path that Christ laid out, one of love, compassion, forgiveness and service, and we draw much comfort and sustenance from praying to this compassionate Christ, who is so deeply human and quietly Divine.

Yet our hearts and souls also reverberate to the image of God as Spirit that is roiling within us unceasingly, sustaining us, giving us life, moving us forward. Images of this progenitive Spirit can be found throughout the Old and New Testaments, in Native American religions, in Earth Goddess cultures and in nature-based religions. In the Bahai religion, originally an offshoot of Islam, all the great Gods and prophets are viewed as variations of the same "One Spirit."

"Spirit" is a powerful image of the Divine and an increasingly popular one today, since it has remained unfettered with the patriarchal and exclusionary connotations of "Father," "Lord" and even God.

When we pray, Spirit is an especially potent image of the Divine on which to focus. It moves us away from images of God that are framed in human terms, and therefore limiting and even self-serving, to an imageless form of the Divine that arises spontaneously within our hearts, and with whom we can have a deep, diverse and unlimited relationship. And prayer, as we shall soon learn, is all about relationship with God, regardless of the images and names we use to build that relationship.

Call it Nature, Fate, Fortune: all
these are names of the one and selfsame
God.

SENECA

All are but parts of one stupendous
whole. . . .

ALEXANDER POPE

A GOD BY ANY OTHER NAME . . .

Call God Abba, Adonai, Allah, Atman, Jehovah, Yah-
weh, Buddha, Brahma, Vishnu, Christ, Elohim, Godhead,
Tao, One Spirit, Holy Ghost, Mohammed, Father Sky, Tam
Apo, Wakan Tanka.

Call God Sophia, Mary, Mother Divine, Devi, Eve, Lilith,
Great Mother, Oya, Hokmah, Shang–ti, Shakti, Shekhinah, Tara, Dakini, Gaia, Kuan–yin, Kali.

Call God Divinity, Wisdom, Wonder, Compassion,
Light, Loving Kindness, Divine Breath, Spirit, Supreme
Intelligence, Great Mystery, Higher Power, Beloved, Other,
Earth, Fire, Wind, Eternal One, the Unnameable, the Ineffable.

These are but a few of the many names and images of
the Divine to whom others have prayed. No doubt you
can add more names and images to the list, perhaps ones
that have a special meaning to you: Brother, Sister, Darkness, Abyss, Void, Beauty, Magnificence.

In our prayer lives, we tend to focus on images of God
that feel familiar and comfortable to us—Allah, Abba,
Jesus, Mary, Kali, Wisdom—or that fulfill a personal need,
desire or aspect of ourselves—Mother, Father, Sophia,
Loving Kindness, Compassionate One.

The value of using familiar images of the Divine in our
prayer life is that they quickly anchor us in sacred ground
and provide us with easy access to a known God with

whom we can easily commune. And if we are committed to and openhearted in our prayer life, these familiar images of God may in time provide a pathway for exploring an even deeper relationship with a more mysterious Divinity, with whom we can fully explore all the hidden recesses of our hearts.

The danger of using familiar images of the Divine is that we may come too easily to believe that they are in fact the "real thing." In effect, we box "our" God into a neat and definable space that serves some particular purpose of ours. Since we can't conceive of God's true nature, which is infinitely more grand and more indefinable than we can possibly imagine, our familiar images of God may have the effect of ultimately limiting our knowledge of a greater and more encompassing Divinity.

He who desires to see the living God
face to face should not seek Him in the
empty firmament of his mind, but in
human love.

FEODOR DOSTOEVSKY

HOW TO RE-ENVISION
THE DIVINE IMAGE IN PRAYER

To begin the task of re-imagining the Divine, theologian Dennis J. Billy, C.S.S.R., says we first need to increase our awareness of the Divine's living presence around us, so that we are open to the variety of ways the Divine is manifested. Billy suggests three ways to expand our awareness of a living God:

Image Fasting

"Image fasting" is just like fasting from food to clean out our systems. With image fasting, we consciously make an effort to reduce the impact of all the riotous media images in our lives, whether they be in television, film, newspapers, the radio. This constant bombardment of modern media images is like psychic pollution, and it can have the effect of dulling our spiritual sensibilities and making it impossible to imagine a deeper Divinity. By image fasting on a regular basis, we create quiet and sacred spaces around us, so that we are more receptive to the presence of God and to the different ways God reaches out to us.

Theological Reflection

When we engage in theological reflection, we look at the many images of the Divine that we hold dear, and examine how each one directly affects our lives and the way we think and behave on a day-to-day basis. Again, such reflection, when done consciously and conscientiously, opens us up to the varied ways the Divine moves in and out of our lives.

Imageless Prayer

In imageless prayer, we put aside our familiar and comfortable images of the Divine, and simply "be" with God. Sitting, kneeling or standing in a quiet room or place, we consciously empty our minds of preconceived thoughts and images and allow God to move unbidden through us, opening our hearts to radically new images of the Divine and taking us along on unimaginable journeys into the mysterious realm of the sacred.

This journey to and with an imageless God is not for the fainthearted. It can be a lonely and darkly mysterious trek across unknown borders and through unreadable terrain. But ultimately, as we progress and mature through prayer, meeting God on God's terms and letting God be God will become our greatest joy and deepest satisfaction.

Many have used meditation to first conjure up and sit with the imageless Divine. Before we move on to the how and why of prayer, then, let's take a look at the role meditation plays along the journey to prayer.

PART ONE

How to Pray

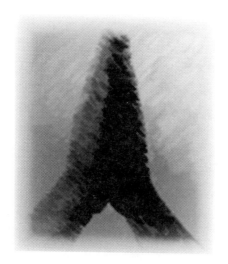

1

What Is Meditation?

∞

Silence is the garden of meditation.

ALI

T his is a book about prayer and about how to pray, so why do we begin by looking at meditation first?

We look at meditation first because, ironically enough, many people who seek spiritual growth know more about meditation, and about Eastern meditation techniques and practices, than they do about the prayers and prayer practices in various Western traditions. In fact, over the last thirty years, meditation has come to be seen by some as a superior or more enlightened form of devotion than prayer, and has even replaced the practice of prayer in many people's lives.

This has happened, in part, because some Westerners find the traditional prayers they learned by rote as children either without spiritual resonance or uncomfortably restrictive in their patriarchal origins, language and worship of a male God.

But even those Westerners who follow traditions such as Hinduism, Buddhism and Taoism—where meditation is viewed as fundamental to spiritual enlightenment—are still less aware of, or are less inclined to practice, the other devotional aspects of these religions, which include an abundance of verbal prayers. Hinduism, Buddhism, Sufism and Taoism, to name just a few Eastern spiritual traditions, have rich histories of verbal prayer and devotion. But though there are hundreds of books on these traditions' meditation techniques, there are very few books extolling their parallel practices of prayer and devotional ritual.

On the other side of the spectrum, many Westerners were never taught, and are only now beginning to discover and appreciate the significant history, role and spiritual power of Christian and Jewish meditation practices, particularly those of the Eastern Orthodox branch of Christianity and the Kabbalistic sect of Judaism.

We also begin with meditation first because, as we shall soon discover, its techniques can be invaluable in preparing the body, mind and heart spiritually for the practice of prayer. Meditation can also serve as a gentle pathway through rote prayers and traditions that have lost their meaning and power to the ecstatic, freeform and spontaneous prayers of the heart that arise from deep within our souls in adoration of the Divine.

Prayer is when you talk to God;
meditation is when you listen to God.

DIANA ROBINSON

Defining Meditation:
Many Things to Many People

It's important to point out at the start that what people call "meditation" is in fact many things to many people and to many cultures. Among those people and cultures, meditation is sometimes viewed as prayer, or at least a prelude to prayer, but many other times it is not. Prayer, in turn, has its meditative aspects—recollection, reflection and contemplation, for example—which we will discuss briefly in this chapter and more extensively in chapter 2.

Prayer, however, is usually markedly different in focus from meditation. Some meditation practices foster, often inadvertently, an absorption with self and self alone, even when the ultimate goal is union with a higher consciousness.

Prayer is always focused on communion with the Divine Other, who is greater than self. Thus meditation most resembles prayer when it shares with it the singular aim of having a relationship with God. When that happens, meditation and prayer can be regarded as separate but equally powerful links to the Divine.

Generally, though, when people talk specifically of meditation, they usually mean one of two types: a non-religious or secular meditation that is aimed at physical, mental and emotional self-improvement; or a spiritually based meditation that is wisdom- or God-centered and aimed at increasing both spiritual self-awareness and awareness of a Divine Presence. Let's look at each of these types of meditation by first generally defining what meditation is.

Does one really have to fret about enlightenment? No matter what road I travel, I'm going home.

SHINSHO

NONSPIRITUAL VERSUS SPIRITUAL MEDITATION

Meditation is usually defined as any of a group of practices that have as a common goal the quieting of the mind and body through focused and nonanalytical attention to a single object, sensation, word, thought or movement. These might be a candle, a flower, an icon, a drawing, the breath, a repeated word or phrase (mantra), a chant, an idea, a line of scriptural text, an inner visualization, or even walking and eating.

Repeatedly using a disciplined and focused attention on the same object, thought, sensation, word or movement during meditation will, over time, still the mind and clear it of random, racing, jumbled thoughts and anxieties. This in turn relaxes our bodies, soothes our emotions, and refocuses and empowers our mental energy. Not only can we perceive certain things more clearly and in a more detached, nonemotional way—including our own inner workings and relationship with self and with others—but we also become more openhearted and receptive to the presence and voice of the Divine stirring within us.

The spiritual power of meditation has been venerated in all religious traditions for millennia. The secular form of meditation, concerned primarily with purely physical and mental benefits, is a Western phenomenon of only the last thirty years.

*Meditation is a mental discipline that
enables us to do one thing at a time.*

MAX PICARD

Nonspiritual or Secular Meditation

The bestselling book, *The Relaxation Response* by Herbert Benson, published over twenty years ago, popularized meditation as a tool for managing and reducing stress, improving physical and mental health and performance, increasing happiness and creating a sense of inner peace. Later proponents of meditation's medical benefits, including Jon Kabat-Zinn and Joan Borysenko, demonstrated that meditation was a powerful aid in helping manage pain, enhance healing and strengthen immunity.

In the last three decades, secular meditation has steadily moved into the arenas of medicine, business, education, sports and the creative arts. Cardiologists recommend meditation to their patients with heart disease to help reduce stress and anxiety. Many large corporations have introduced meditation techniques to their employees, both to reduce job-related stress and to increase productivity. Students and performing artists meditate to focus concentration, enhance memory and increase creativity. Athletes in a variety of sports meditate to improve physical performance and mental endurance on the playing fields.

Even young children are meditating, but perhaps not for the right reasons! Last summer a friend of ours invited us to watch his nine-year-old daughter play in a soccer game. Much to everyone's amazement, the opposing team didn't spend their thirty-minute warm-up period doing stretches and laps around the field. Instead, they sat in a circle with their coach and meditated silently for twenty minutes. Many onlookers giggled, including members of our home team. The opposing team ignored the laughter and went on to play masterfully and win!

However, whether these little nine- and ten-year-olds had any idea of the spiritual dimensions of their meditation is debatable. And the promotion of meditation by adults to children as a device to "beat the other guy" is questionable at best.

That is not to say that secular meditation doesn't have a powerful and wonderful place in people's lives. The physical, mental and emotional benefits of nonspiritual meditation, particularly meditation techniques that reduce stress, alleviate pain and promote a sense of well-being, are inherently good. Even more, the increased awareness and inner stillness and receptivity that meditation promotes may awaken in the secular practitioner a spiritual hunger for something greater than self. Secular meditation may indeed become a doorway to the greater mystery that lies within and outside self.

Still, much modern meditation practice, particularly meditation promulgated at cult-like centers with all-too-fallible human leaders, seems to encourage self-absorption and material gain rather than selflessness and relationship with God and others. And that is definitely not spiritually based meditation. Instead, places that promote that kind of meditation are usually engaged in what the fine spiritual writer, mystic and retreat leader David Cooper calls "hula hoop spirituality," where instant enlightenment and tranquility are guaranteed in just one weekend.

Feeling good, improving oneself and getting what one wants from life also seem to be the aims of the many secular meditators who gather in large groups at expensive retreats to encourage one another in their self-oriented pursuits. Such groups and their leaders have been the subjects of much criticism and exposés, and no doubt they represent a minority of meditation practitioners. (And let us not forget that prayer, too, can be manipulated for ill gain.)

Still, the self-promoting type of contemporary meditation described above can be particularly harmful because it can throw a long and dark shadow on other spiritually based meditation practices—and centers—that have deep and varied roots in both Western and Eastern traditions, and that are replete with other beautiful devotional practices, including prayer and ritual. Self-promoting meditation-for-the-masses not only has nothing to do with devotion and prayer, but it shares little with the historical origins of true spiritual meditation, which had its birth, in both the East and West, among small groups of prophets and pilgrims who withdrew from society, for the most part, and lived in solitary, isolated, even desolate places.

In quietude and solitude before the face
of God our souls can hear better than at any other time.

O. Hallesby

Spiritual Meditation

All spiritual meditation can be viewed as an attempt through focused attention to break down and discard those parts of our selves that are "false" and thus separate us from true wisdom, compassionate relationship with others and a deep, heartfelt union with the Divine. Meditation is both an inward sifting of the sands of our heart and soul to discover who we are in relation to God and the world, and an outward reaching toward God for love, insight, consolation and renewal.

Every major religious and spiritual tradition practices some form of meditation, either as devotion to the Divine or as a means of understanding the greater wisdom and truths of the universe.

Hindu and Taoist meditation practices predate all others, and involve meditation techniques devoted to gods and to saints as well as to the universal ideals of compassion, wisdom and understanding as a means of following the true path or way (Tao) of enlightenment.

Jewish meditation practices can be found throughout the Old Testament, and in Deuteronomy in particular. Ancient Jews were instructed to take the beautiful words of the beloved Shema, the greatest of Jewish prayers, directly into their hearts and souls and to recite them there unceasingly: "The Lord is our God, the Lord alone!" This was one of the earliest forms of monologistic prayer or meditation, in which a word or phrase is repeated over and over as the focus of the meditation.

Buddhist meditation techniques, which began flourishing a few hundred years before the birth of Christ, eventually evolved into myriad meditative practices. Primary among them were meditation practices aimed at attaining enlightenment by focusing on the ideals of loving-kindness (metta meditation), insight or wisdom (vipassana meditation), or tranquility (samatha meditation), while paying focused attention to the inward and outward flow of the breath.

Fourth- and fifth-century Christians, called the Desert Fathers and Mothers, who were dissatisfied with the way Christianity was being interpreted by the mainstream, left

their cosmopolitan cities in Greece and Rome to seek the
true wisdom of holy fathers, or Abbas, who had retreated
to the deserts of Syria and Egypt to commune directly
with God. These Desert Fathers and Mothers later
recorded and carried back to their cities the first formalized techniques for Christian meditation. These techniques were similar to the Jewish meditation techniques
of the Old Testament in that they focused on two simple
phrases that were to be repeated unceasingly in the
heart: "O God, come to my assistance; O Lord, make haste
to help me."

It is hard to wait and press and pray, and
hear no voice, but stay till God answers.

E. M. Bounds

Silent Meditation and Monologistic Meditation

Silent meditation that uses the breath as a focus for
quieting the mind is one of the most popular spiritual
meditation techniques, and is practiced particularly
among many Buddhist sects. However, it is a difficult
meditation technique to master, particularly when you
are just starting out on your spiritual journey. The wild
and irrational ramblings of the mind and petty demands
of the ego are powerful distractions when observed in
solitary silence, and thus breath–centered meditation
may have the disadvantage for the neophyte of too
readily leading one into self-centered observation.

Monologistic or mantra–type meditation, however, is
almost as popular as breath–centered meditation, and has
the advantage, through the use of single words or short

phrases, of immediately establishing a link "outside" one-self to a greater Other. This can help the practitioner achieve a meditative state more easily and thus become more readily receptive to the presence of God within and without.

Further, the techniques and focus of monologistic or mantra meditation are remarkably similar across diverse cultures and religious traditions, so when we practice this form of meditation we are all divinely linked with one another across cultures, countries and centuries.

God enters by a private door into every individual.

RALPH WALDO EMERSON

Monologistic or Mantra Meditation Around the World

The original Christian desert meditation of the fourth and fifth centuries, which focused on repeating a phrase from the Psalms in the Old Testament, had, by the four-teenth century, evolved into the famous "Jesus Prayer" meditation of the Eastern Christian Church, and the phrase that was now repeated unceasingly was taken from the New Testament:

Jesus Christ, have mercy on me, a sinner.

But the Eastern Church also had been strongly influ-enced by the occupying Muslim culture, and the way they practiced the Jesus Prayer was quite similar to the thirteenth-century Sufi Muslim practice of *Dhikr Allah,* the chanting of any of the ninety-nine beautiful names of God.

The *dhikr* form of meditation is, in turn, similar to the meditation practices of Kabbalistic Judaism, which arose in the Middle Ages and have as their focus *devekut*, or mystical union with *Ayn Sof* (the Infinite), also by repeating the names of God in mantra-like fashion.

The *dhikr* meditation practice was modeled on the twelfth-century Buddhist devotional practice of *nembutsu*, found in the Pure Land sect of Buddhism, which consisted of a continual reciting of the words *Namu Amida Butsu* (Veneration to the Buddha Amitabha).

Nembutsu itself borrowed heavily from the ancient Hindu form of monologistic meditation called *japa* or *japam* (to "whisper" or "murmur"), which entailed the continual repetition of Brahma's many names.

All of these forms of mantra-like or monologistic meditations have two primary aims: to invite the Divine into one's being through adoration; and to increase one's awareness of the presence of God within us and in the world around us. That the aims and techniques of these meditative practices are so remarkably similar is a profound testament to the spiritual universality of meditation practices, and to the fact that we all share the same yearnings for Divine connectedness. We are, after all, brothers and sisters in the same Divine family. However differently we look and feel and experience our personal realities, however contrasting our views of the Ultimate Reality, we all turn in the same direction, with the same words upon our lips, in search of the face of God.

You are used to listening to the buzz
of the world, but now is the time to
develop the inner ear that listens to
the inner world. It is time to have a
foot in each world, and it can be done.

ST. BARTHOLOMEW

FROM MEDITATION TO
PRAYER AND CONTEMPLATION

To go back to the theme with which we started this chapter, meditation isn't better than prayer or a replacement for prayer. It is but one point on a spiritual continuum of searching and growing into God's presence. If anything, meditation is in fact a prelude to prayer in our spiritual evolution. It is the fertile ground into which we first plough the seeds of our yearning, searching selves.

We can liken this evolution to what happens to a baby as she grows through life from infancy to elder status. In many ways, if she is to grow into the person she was meant to be, if she is to evolve successfully through each phase of growing up and growing old, her life will be a series of poignant stages where she is either listening, talking or simply being.

As a baby, she is all receptivity: eyes bright and wide open, a trusting heart, a facile mind ready to absorb all that she needs to learn to engage with the world. She listens, she watches, she waits to make her move. This is meditation—this listening, watching, waiting.

Then, trusting that the people around her are there to stay, to help, to protect, and having learned just enough to get their attention, the baby makes her move.

She reaches out in language, she speaks, she engages the others, she forms relationships, she learns even more about herself and about the others. First she does this at home. Later she will do it in school. Much later she will do this in work, in society, in love, in family. This is prayer—this trustful reaching out to others through language, this attempt at relationship with others, this constant learning about self, about others, about the world. Most of her adult life may be a journey of prayer for this child, a never-ending reaching out, searching for new words, new meanings and deeper relationships.

In the fullness of her maturity, if life has mostly been happy and good and kind, this child's reaching out and searching will have been rewarded. Life has meaning, her relationships are solid, her sense of self is strong, words are no longer necessary. She can sit in the lushness of her good life, with her faithful others, and simply enjoy the knowledge that she is loved and has someone to love. This is contemplation—this simply being, this purely loving, this confidence in self and in the Other.

From the moment you came into the world
of being, a ladder was placed before you
that you might escape.

Divani Shamsi Tabriz

Meditation is the place where we are wholly receptive, preparing ourselves as sacred ground to be seeded and ploughed, weeded and turned, watered and fed and nourished by the light of the Divine.

Prayer is the place where we walk the readied fields hand-in-hand with the Divine, doing the seeding, the ploughing, the watering, the nourishing, talking together over the noise of the world around us, arguing, crying, braving droughts and windstorms together, but always working together.

In the late autumn of our spiritual lives—which is not necessarily when we are old, but whenever contemplation is possible—we sit at the table with the Divine and drink and eat deeply of the lush and bountiful harvest we have planted together.

Prayer is the ladder, the walkway, the turnaround between meditation and contemplation, when we move from merely watching and waiting for the Divine to calling out God's name in absolute faith that there will be an answer.

Let's move on and take the first step together.

2

What Is Prayer?

∞

Prayer is an all-efficient panoply, a treasure undiminished, a mine which is never exhausted, a sky unobscured by clouds, a heaven unruffled by the storm. It is the root, the fountain, the mother of a thousand blessings.

ST. JOHN CHRYSOSTOM

I n trying to define prayer we meet with paradox, because prayer has been and continues to be different things to different people. It has been alternately described and defined as poetic, pragmatic, ineffable, ecstatic, ordinary, extraordinary, sacred, mundane; the visceral stuff of the everyday, the evanescent vapor of the unknowable; the rarified province of mystics, the earthy domain of simple souls; the thing, the process, the mystery in which we are spiritually grounded, exalted, humbled, ennobled, beloved, abandoned, transformed, protected and renewed by a power greater than ourselves yet part of ourselves.

And this is just a small sampling of how prayer has been viewed by diverse people and cultures throughout the ages, for prayer has been with us since the beginning of time—since that first moment when prehistoric man and woman lifted their hands and eyes to the darkening sky of a forbidding landscape, cried out for deliverance and heard, incredibly, something deeply, infinitely hopeful answering within their hearts.

Prayer has been called other things, too. For St. Clement of Alexandria, prayer was simply a "conversation" with God; for St. Therese of Lisieux, it was "an upward leap of the heart, an untroubled glance toward heaven." Nobel prize-winning surgeon Alexis Carrel believed prayer was both "a cry of distress" and a "hymn of love," and J. Edgar Hoover viewed prayer as the "greatest means of trapping the infinite resources of God." German theologian Dietrich Bonhoeffer defined prayer as a means to "find the way to God and to speak with Him, whether the heart is full or empty," while historian Thomas Carlyle saw prayer as the "deepest impulse of the soul of man."

Among Jews, prayer is a *mitzvah*, an essential commandment, a "humble answer to the inconceivable surprise of living." Being a Muslim and praying are considered synonymous in the faith of Islam. And Hindus regard praying as essential to the spiritual life as breathing is to the physical life. For many devotional Buddhists, every act, every gesture, every moment is a prayer. And among some Native Americans, every movement is a prayer.

Prayer, what St. John Chrysostom rightly calls an "all-efficient panoply," has also been described as bliss, divine communion, a golden key to heaven, a fortress against evil, a metaphysical gymnasium in which we stretch our spiritual muscles, an anchor during emotional storms, a refuge from loneliness and despair, food for the soul, a cry in the wilderness, an explosion of joy and the ultimate act of love.

Prayer in its simplest definition is merely a wish turned God-ward.

PHILLIPS BROOKS

CALLED BY GOD:
PRAYER AS LOVING RELATIONSHIP

Just a brief look at the prayers in Part Two of this book confirms the great diversity of emotions, thoughts and attitudes around the process of prayer.

The small sample of prayers we've included vibrate with the voices of joy, adoration, rapture, sorrow, love, anger, desire and regret. They whisper and they shout. They stutter and they strut. They are hesitant and confident, humble and exalted. They are as rich and complex, simple and straightforward, as the human hearts from which they spring.

As different as they are, though, all those who raise their voices in these prayers share one striking commonality. They have no doubt to whom they are talking. They are talking to God. More extraordinary, God has given them this very conviction as an outright gift. Even when hesitant and humbled, therefore, these prayerful voices cast their hopes, petitions, joys, sorrows, gratitude and most of all, love into dark and unknown waters, with the absolute belief that a God they cannot see or touch will catch their words, cherish them and love the one who spoke the words.

In the beginning and in the end, then, prayer is an act of consummate love between human and Divine, mortal and immortal. Buoyed by faith and commitment, prayer is the purest, most passionate relationship we will ever experience.

Fittingly, the Divine relationship we experience in prayer shares many of the ingredients of our best human relationships, only raised to a more profound level of experience: deep communication, steadfast commitment,

absolute fidelity, pure passion, quiet humility, unconditional love. But there are other ways in which the relationship between God and us—through prayer—is
markedly different from relationships in the human realm.

The very best and utmost in attainment in this
life is to remain still and let God act and
speak in thee.

MEISTER ECKHART

Prayer: *We Are Called*

Perhaps the most striking difference between prayer
and human encounters is that the prayer relationship is
one we don't—indeed, we can't—initiate ourselves, however paradoxical that may sound. God does the initiating
because God is there before us, waiting, even before the
idea of prayer is part of our consciousness. God speaks to
us from within, extending the invitation to prayer, arms
wide. God does the calling, not us. We answer God; it's
not the other way around. God waits, we show up.

Once we start showing up, of course we have to bring
faith and commitment to prayer and be willing to practice making it a part of our daily lives. But that is all we
are called to do; the field in which we will plant our
prayers has already been tilled and turned by God, who
waits for our arrival.

Divine Prevenience

In classical theological terms, the fact that God anticipates
our need for relationship, and then generously and

lovingly invites us to explore that relationship in prayer, is called "divine prevenience." In the simplest of terms, this means that God is always anticipating us—our needs, our actions, our petitions—always waiting for us to answer the invitation to prayer and relationship.

Contrary to many people's notions about prayer, then, is the fact that *we* are *asked* to pray by the Divine; we are not *moved* to pray by our own desires, however sincere they may be. Prayer is neither a spiritual exercise nor a human convenience. It is a human necessity and Divine commandment. We hunger and thirst for a connection with something infinitely greater and more encompassing than ourselves and our human relationships. The Divine answers with a call to intimate communion in prayer.

Being able to accept that God initiates our praying and is always there for us—before, during and after the experience—should be a comfort and beacon as we begin a life of prayer. What a relief to know that we don't have to go searching for God; God is already there. We don't have to whip ourselves into a spiritual frenzy to pray; we are born with the instinct to pray (though it helps sometimes to have props around to keep us rooted in the here and now. We speak about this in chapter 4). We do not have to retreat from the world to live prayerfully either. If God is everywhere—and God is—and the opportunity to pray is everywhere—and it is—we can pray anytime and anywhere: to the thrumming of cicadas or the screeching of train wheels; in a pine forest or in a baseball stadium; on our knees or on our toes.

The Fallacy of Trying to Anticipate God

Amazingly, the "anticipatory" nature of the Divine is a problem for some of us, not a comfort. We humans are freewheeling, self-seeking, independent-minded, cause-and-effect creatures who relish quick answers and instant gratification. The notion that we can't "mold and shape" prayer, and therefore God, to our specifications, our convenience, our schedules, and our needs, wants and demands is frustrating to some of us who don't know how to sit and wait for God's call, let alone listen and respond.

For others of us, driven by ego and intellect, consumed with notions of self-determination and self-actualization, the notion of God's prevenience can become an insurmountable spiritual obstacle. The ego, run rampant and wholly self-centered, is a powerful foe of sincere prayer. It tells us that even in prayer we can have it our way and do it our way, without the intercession of the Divine.

The Fallacy of Turning Prayer into a Competition

Willfulness, too, is a foe of prayer. Many of us believe that prayer is something we do with great effort, on our own, after much thought, planning and rationalization. We view prayer as a challenge with which we must struggle until we get it right. Sometimes we read and talk more about prayer and spirituality than we actually practice either. Too often we make prayer an intellectual exercise, relegating it to the passionless borders of the mind. Or we turn prayer into a spiritual competition, where winning bestows celestial favors and superior enlightenment. When we don't get what we ask for in prayer, either we abandon prayer entirely, seeing it as an empty gesture, or we consider ourselves spiritual failures.

You can do more than pray after you have prayed,
but you cannot do more than pray until you have prayed.

A. J. GORDON

Heeding the Call to Prayer

Prayer is not an obstacle to be overcome, a competition to be won, an object to be manipulated or an intellectual concept to be analyzed. Prayer can't be broken down and neatly boxed in self-help wrappings so that you can take it home with you, quickly put it together and get down to the work of praying. That's one of the reasons that most books that attempt to explain prayer are rather slim volumes indeed.

It is difficult to teach prayer and impossible to manufacture or force it into service for our own convenience. Still, we are a people who've become accustomed to fighting for everything we want, and prayer is no different. We think if we try hard enough, we will "nail" prayer like all the other hard-won accomplishments and talismans of our corporal lives. And when we "nail" prayer, we will then enjoy the manifold gifts some New Age writers tell us that prayer inevitably bestows: healing, prosperity, marriage, success and ecstatic states of being.

This simply isn't so. All great spiritual traditions point to one irrevocable fact: However hard we beat our breasts, prostrate ourselves or wave our fists at the sky, the exquisite union of the human and Divine in a relationship of prayer is an unmerited *gift* from God, not a *thing* we acquire under our own power. We are *invited* into the Divine relationship, each and every one of us, by God and no one else. And we are extended the invitation whether our hearts are open to it or not.

As for prayer's rewards, they are many—but not necessarily the romance and riches promised by some commercial purveyors of prayer. Honest prayer can never be a vehicle for satisfying our desires. Indeed, very often we don't get what we pray for. And sometimes that's a good thing.

Nor is the prayer experience always deep and meaningful, ecstatic and joy-filled: There will be long, dry stretches of desert during our prayer lives and occasional dark nights of the soul when we lose the hand of God in the darkness. Because prayer is ineffable, because it is a journey guided by a power greater than ourselves, because it is as unique and mysterious as each individual who prays, we cannot predict where prayer will take us or understand why we are taken. And sometimes prayer takes us to lonely, empty places where we must confront who we are at our most humanly fragile core.

Your invitation to pray is a Divine call to a very particular, very personal relationship with God. No one else will have the same relationship with the Divine that you do. Your prayer relationship will be private, intimate and uniquely yours. It is an exclusive communion between yourself and the Divine, powerfully framed in shared love and mutuality. Once you sanctify this relationship with your prayers and your presence, you will never be able to comfortably ignore or abandon it again.

All we need to enter this sacred realm of prayer is an open heart and God's guiding hand. When we open our hearts and extend our hands, we find ourselves inevitably yielding to a gentle siren song within that beckons us to know and love God like we never have before.

Some of us hear and heed this call sooner and more enthusiastically than do others; some ignore the call entirely. But because this call to love and relationship with the Divine is extended to everyone, all of us are born with an instinct to pray, to bow our heads, to extend our hands. Whether we honor that instinct, ignore it or belittle it as beneath our rational intellects, it is there nonetheless, waiting to be sated. And we pray far more than we realize, even the most stubborn of us. Every silent or half-murmured wish, hope or cry for a healthy child, restored health, fair weather, good crops, full bellies, safe trips, lasting peace and true happiness is a prayer to something greater than ourselves, whether we name it prayer and God or not.

Finally, because we both come from and carry within us the very God who calls us to pray, prayer becomes both a natural expression of our inner divinity and an unbreakable link to the eternal Godhead. We know when we are being called and when we are on the brink of prayer because deep within our hearts there begins to grow a tender but gnawing yearning for a love, a union and a knowledge beyond anything the earth has to offer us. If we fan the fires of this yearning, we are inevitably led to pray.

Prayer is the incense of a holy heart
Rising to God from bruised and broken things,
When kindled by the Spirit's burning breath
And upward borne by faith's ascending wings.

A. B. Simpson

Prayer: Yearning to Answer and Learning to Listen

Many mystics, saints, theologians and ordinary folk who have embarked on passionate prayer lives all acknowledge that before a prayerful word is ever spoken, we remain for some time—maybe even years—in a state of hungry yearning for connection with the Divine.

At first we probably won't recognize that the yearning is about connecting with God or about joining the Divine in the relationship of prayer.

We may, however, suddenly feel emotionally confused, unhappy with our lives as they are. Where before we were easily satisfied with simple pleasures and shiny talismans of success, now there may be a poignant emptiness at our emotional centers that we never seem able to fill.

Perhaps it's useful to think of this pre-prayer state as the adolescence of our spiritual lives. Before the yearning begins, we have spent much of our time, energy and willfulness in growing up, accumulating knowledge, getting to know ourselves and others, forming relationships, finding a career, settling down with family, acquiring money and possessions, growing comfortable in our little worlds—including growing comfortable with or discarding the religious or spiritual traditions of our parents.

Then, often quite suddenly, the feeling that something important but ineffable is missing from our lives hits us squarely in our spiritual solar plexus, in our hearts. We are hungry for something but we're not sure what. We walk through life with a sense of discontent and unconnectedness. Our spirits are unsettled. We are not as whole as we thought we were. Something vital and life-sustaining is absent from our souls. We are achingly incomplete. We search for the missing piece of ourselves, and sometimes we catch a glimpse of it, evanescent, out of the corner of our eye. Then it is gone in a flash.

This spiritual turmoil is yearning for the Divine, and it is as much a gift from God as is the act of prayer itself. All great things, ideas and, most of all, great relationships begin with an indefinable but fiery passion. Yearning is our passion for union with the Divine in prayer.

Sometimes we must sit with our yearning for quite a while, sifting through our preconceived notions of who we think we are, of how we feel about ourselves, the Divine, the world, of who or what we believe God to be. We need to ask ourselves what still works for us spiritually, and what doesn't.

We cannot begin any new relationship—let alone the leap into the unknown that the prayer relationship is— unless we shed or at least reexamine some of our old beliefs and preconceptions. In prayer we are also called to a rare kind of surrender of self; we are asked to suspend all our disbeliefs and trust wholly in the Divine's will for us. So the time of yearning is also a time to reexamine our faith and our capacity to trust in a power greater than ourselves, and to put our lives into that power's hands.

While we yearn for connection, for relationship, for prayer, for the Divine; while we divest ourselves of those character traits and emotional beliefs that are encumbrances to prayer; while we learn to sit, however uncomfortably, with our hungry yearning for the Indefinable and the Unknown, an extraordinary thing happens. We learn to wait with a more open heart. We learn to listen with new ears. We begin to hear a new inner voice that is both our self and yet not our self, and we come to under-stand that God is calling us.

During our yearning, we learn to feel in new ways and to listen to the Divine in new ways. We reaffirm our faith and trust in God (though it will continue to grow in leaps and bounds throughout our prayer life). We sit and wait, we develop patience and more faith. Suddenly, when the yearning has become almost unbearable, we call out our-selves with new voices and renewed faith, and as surely as a current of electricity flies though the circuitry when we flip a switch on a wall, so, too, do our new voices and full hearts fly directly to the Divine.

Prayer is exhaling the spirit of man and inhaling the spirit of God.

EDWIN KEITH

Prayer: Answering the Call and Learning to Speak

Simplistic as it sounds, if you want to pray, you will pray, with words or without words. There is no secret for-mula or arcane trick to praying and praying well. As we discussed earlier, we are all born with the instinct to pray. Indeed, many spiritual masters say that if we can breathe, we can pray. In fact, the Old Testament tells us we were formed by God's very breath. We come into the world with a deep inhalation and we leave the world with one last great exhalation. In many ways, our entire life between those breaths is a prayer. We are, in the final analysis, prayer. The Divine prayed us into being where before there was nothing but darkness and abyss. We thank the Divine for our being by answering back with our own nascent prayers.

Living well and righteously may be prayer enough for some people. Others of us want to go deeper and know the Divine as intimately as possible. We can. God is always calling. If we have sat with our yearning, imbued ourselves with renewed faith, learned to listen for the voice of the Divine in the stillness of expectant hearts, we will find the way to answer God in prayer. Again, there are many ways to pray, and we discuss some of them in the next section. The select prayers we list in Part Two of the book are also meant to open your heart more fully to the process of prayer and to encourage you to find faith-filled words of your own.

What we need to bring to prayer is commitment. And we commit ourselves to the Divine through the relationship of prayer by practicing praying regularly; by showing up even when we are empty and heavy-hearted, angry and hurt; by being willing to live through the inevitable spells of silence and arid desert; by never abandoning the Divine because the process becomes too hard or frightening or we become indifferent and dull-hearted.

We are a people hungry for spiritual nourishment, yet for too long we have put prayer on the theological back burner in deference to more dramatic and colorful rituals. It's time to return to prayer. Knowing the Divine through the relationship of prayer is not a waivable option; all great traditions tell us that prayer, habitual prayer, is the single most important component of our spiritual lives.

Prayer is invoking the impossible.

JACK W. HAYFORD

Prayer . . . an attitude of heart, which God recognizes as prayer
whether it manifests itself in quiet thinking,
in sighing or in audible words.

O. HALLESBY

FINDING A PRAYERFUL PATH: WAYS TO PRAY

There are as many ways to pray as there are individuals who pray. Just as we communicate with and relate to
one another in distinctly individualistic ways, so, too, do
we pray uniquely. We find a mode of prayer that is comfortable for us, that resonates strongly with who and
what we are and what our image of the Divine is. Sometimes, depending on our needs and state of mind, we
even practice different ways to pray at the same time.

There are four basic ways to pray: wordless prayer or
contemplation; reflective or discursive prayer; verbal
prayer; and prayer through action.

It is necessary for us to withdraw at regular intervals
and enable our souls to attain that
quietude and inward composure which are
essential if we would hear the voice of God.

O. HALLESBY

Contemplative Prayer

Contemplative prayer is the wordless prayer of silence and stillness that arises and is centered in the heart. In Eastern traditions it is called meditation. In Western traditions it has various names: the prayer of silence or solitude, centering prayer, the prayer of presence or the prayer of awareness.

Silence and solitude are part and parcel of contemplative prayer. We need a quiet place where we can calm both body and mind and be undisturbed by the outside world. As we empty our mind of all the scattered and random free-flying thoughts and concerns of everyday life, we slowly, gently and exclusively focus our heart's love and attention on the Divine and the Divine alone.

It is helpful when first beginning contemplative prayer to use a word or mantra, an image, or the breath as a focus for quieting our minds and fixing our inner vision on the presence of God. As we sink deeper into quiet and into relationship with the Divine, we can begin to let go of our focus and simply sit or kneel, bathed in the glory of Divinity's presence. We ask nothing and we want nothing, but to be with God in mutual love.

Many spiritual teachers and practitioners view contemplation as a higher form of prayer, a natural spiritual progression from the basic need for words to communicate with the Divine to the more sublime ability simply to sit quietly with God in adoration and humility.

But in fact, contemplative prayer can be an excellent preparation for verbal prayer, for it frees us from rote prayers and the secular connotations of familiar words. When we are just starting out on the prayer journey, the all-too-familiar words of some verbal prayers have a myriad of associations that can, paradoxically, limit and constrain the dimensions of our prayer relationship.

In the quiet of contemplative prayer we discover a new voice within, and with it new words to express our devotion to the Divine.

Prayer is the contemplation of the facts of life from the highest point of view.

RALPH WALDO EMERSON

Reflective Prayer

Reflective prayer is also wordless, but it is prayer that uses the mind, or more specifically, the thought processes of the mind, as a route to the heart of God.

In reflective prayer—also called rumination or "divine reading" (*lectio divina*)—we first read a short passage from a sacred text or a spiritual work. We approach this reading of sacred or spiritual words with the same reverence and commitment as we would approach the practice of contemplation or verbal prayer. We also need quiet and a defined space and time in which we can reflect on our readings, undisturbed by the temptations of the outside world.

The text we select should be read slowly and with absolute attentiveness. The aim of reflective prayer is to invite the sacred words we read to take deep root in our hearts and there have a full and richly textured life of their own separate from the page. We meditate upon these heart-held words, giving them color, movement, new meaning. We search among these living words for precious gems of knowledge and faith, and for the lessons they have to share with us about how to live in God and in the world in new and grace-filled ways.

Often reflective prayer will give rise to uniquely original and deeply meaningful verbal prayer, and many practitioners of reflective prayer also keep a journal nearby to write down any spontaneous prayers or thoughts that arise during their rumination.

The Psalms of the Old Testament are a wonderful source for reflective prayer. Their eloquent beauty captivates our imaginations and rivets our attention, and their universal themes lend themselves to every imaginable human situation and prayerful state.

Reflective prayer may also be practiced with a piece of art or sacred music. The English nun and art historian, Sister Wendy Beckett, has raised to extraordinary levels the practice of using paintings and other artwork as a focus for reflective prayer. Her many books of reflections are themselves sources of great inspiration.

Reflective prayer both enlivens the mind and opens the heart in ways that contemplation and verbal prayer cannot. In essence, we are bringing a third voice into our prayer relationship, a mediating voice of love and wisdom that floats between the Divine and us. Avoid the temptation, however, to make reflective prayer an intellectual exercise. As with all prayer, the aim of reflection is to go deep to the heart and know and love God more fully at the very center of our being.

Prayer is the simplest form of speech
That infant lips can try;

Prayer the sublimest strains that reach
The Majesty on high.

JAMES MONTGOMERY

Verbal Prayer

Praying with words is the way of prayer with which we are most familiar. With very few exceptions, most of us learned some form of prayer, usually by rote memory, as children, whether it was a nighttime blessing or grace before meals.

Verbal prayer, even when the words are familiar, can be innovative and feel new every time we pray. Practitioners of rote, verbal prayers report that as a prayer becomes increasingly familiar to the point where the words come unbidden and unrehearsed, the prayer seems to become a part of the self. It becomes a mantra that gains meaning and depth over time. The well-known Jesus Prayer falls into this category. When one prays without ceasing, "Lord Jesus have mercy on me, a sinner," one enters a type of spiritual depth that can only be reached via this intimacy with words that have become familiar as breath.

On the other hand, the problem with familiar prayers learned by rote is that the words can lose their resonance. Familiarity can breed indifference. Sometimes we can bring back their original meaning by relearning how to say familiar prayers more slowly and with more feeling.

Mature verbal prayer often calls for us to find new words to pray and new meanings for those words. As with contemplative and reflective prayer, preparation, commitment and practice are key to a heartfelt prayer life and to a deep relationship with the Divine. A quiet place and a regular and habitual prayer time are necessary ingredients of good verbal prayer. (We talk more about preparing for prayer, particularly verbal prayer, in chapter 4.)

Quieting the mind and the body are crucial in verbal prayer, as are posture and environment. It is important to feel some connection with the place in which we pray.

Unless your verbal prayer is a "prayer of the heart" like the unceasing Jesus Prayer, it is wise to begin verbal prayer time with some silent and reflective prayer. This helps calm restless thoughts and limbs, and helps frame the moment in reverence and mystery.

Prayer at its best is the expression of the
total life, for all things else being equal,
our prayers are only as powerful as our lives.

A. W. Tozer

Prayer Through Action

Action becomes our prayer when we make a conscious commitment either to make our work our prayer or to carry the wisdom and love we are gifted with in prayer into our daily lives.

It is the rare individual indeed who can make work his or her prayer consistently. Mother Teresa was an extraordinary example. So, too, were Gandhi and Martin Luther King Jr. Some clerics and spiritual teachers, together with individuals involved in peace and social justice efforts, also have the opportunity to turn work into prayer.

All of us, however, can bring the gifts and blessing gleaned in our prayer lives into our relationships with the world. We can bring compassion, tolerance, forgiveness and unconditional love to our work and to our life with family and friends.

The way we pray—contemplatively, reflectively, with words or with actions—is greatly influenced by the type of prayer we are engaged in. Prayers of adoration, for example, lend themselves perfectly to the contemplative format. Prayers of praise or thanksgiving spring to life in verbal prayer. Let's look at some of the different kinds of prayer.

Pray: To address God or a god with adoration, confession, supplication, or thanksgiving; an address (as a petition) to God or a god in word or thought.

MERRIAM WEBSTER'S COLLEGIATE DICTIONARY, TENTH EDITION

It is the heart which experiences God, and not the reason.

BLAISE PASCAL

TYPES OF PRAYER

Traditionally, prayer has been divided into five basic types—adoration, praise, thanksgiving, contrition and petition. Here we also include discussions of two more powerful types of prayer—intercession and oblation.

Just as our human relationships are many-layered fabrics of feelings, needs and wants, so, too, is our prayer relationship with the Divine a multitextured thing.

The breadth and timbre of the voice we bring to prayer will change from day to day. Sometimes we will want simply to adore God and quietly simmer in the exquisite sensation of being in Divine communion. Other times we will want to praise God for the beauty and grace that touches our lives. There will be still other days when we bring to the Divine our thanks for special blessings or our sorrow for a fall from grace. We will also come to our God asking help for ourselves or for another, or we may, as we mature in our prayer life, offer ourselves to the Divine as instruments of God's will, whatever that will may be and wherever it may take us.

Many spiritual teachers suggest that we always begin our prayer time with at least one prayer of adoration, acknowledging the ineffable yet wholly manifest existence of the Divine in everything we see, hear, touch, experience. On the other hand, the great German mystic, Meister Eckhart, believed that if the only prayer we ever said was "thank you," that would be enough.

The truth is, no one prayer is better or purer than another, because all genuine prayer—whether praise or petition, adoration or thanksgiving—rises up from the ever-deepening wells of our love for and belief in the Divine, together with our growing commitment to sanctify our love and faith in the relationship of prayer. So we may give voice in prayer to whatever we are moved to offer the Divine from the altar of our hearts. It is the act of offering that sanctifies the relationship.

Prayer is essentially man standing before his God in wonder,
awe, and humility; man, made in the image of God,
responding to his Maker.

GEORGE APPLETON

Adoration

We lift our voices in prayers of adoration when we kneel at the Divine's feet, utterly transfixed by God's magnificence and by the beauty of life around us—each person, animal, rock, breeze, leaf, insect, strain of music, color of sky and sea—all indelibly imbued with Divinity's love and grace.

We pray in adoration when we are suddenly humbled by the knowledge of the extraordinary and unmerited gift we have received in being held in the arms of the Divine as we pray.

In our prayers of adoration, we simply love God and joyfully affirm the Divine's extraordinary capacity for love, forgiveness and compassion. We revel in the wonder of our grace-filled existence amidst all the Divinity's splendid bounty. We experience a surrender of the ego and a state of "no self" when we adore our God, because God is our only focus then; we are absent, our needs and wants put aside. We lose ourselves in adoring God but find our spirits renewed, if not transformed, by the state of simply being, in love, with God. Thus the very prayers of adoration we offer up become gifts themselves from the Divine, who allows us the powerful experience of knowing what it means to love and give glory unconditionally. God is the absolute focus of our prayerful adoration, and the reward is an unsurpassing sense of happiness and inner peace.

Prayer of Adoration

Take, O Lord, and receive my entire liberty,
my memory, my understanding, and my whole will.
All that I am, all that I have, Thou has given
me, and I will give it back again to Thee to be
disposed of according to Thy good pleasure.
Give me only Thy love and Thy grace; with Thee
I am rich enough. . . .

St. Ignatius Loyola

Though we cannot by our prayers give God any
information, yet we must by our prayers give
Him honor.

Matthew Henry

Praise

Prayers of praise are similar to prayers of adoration, and in fact they are often described together. In both types of prayer, the Divine is the singular focus of our love and attention; we put our egos aside—together with our needs and wants—and simply adore and praise God, for the wonder of the Divine's very being and for the magnificence of God's creations. Prayers of adoration and praise also tend to be brief and simple:

Sanctus, Sanctus, Sanctus (Holy, Holy, Holy)
—or—
We praise you O God, for all your works are wonderful.

There are some subtle differences, however, between the two types of prayer. Prayers of adoration are very much like the silent and sometimes ecstatic states of being experienced in contemplative prayer, when we let God be God and nothing else. We adore God for God's sake, sometimes regardless of the Divine's manifest beauty around us.

Heartfelt prayers of adoration may come more slowly to us. Indeed, we may have to learn how to adore, for it is not a state of being or a feeling that is usual and customary for us. Quiet and stillness may more easily foster our prayers of adoration. Reading the spiritual works of the great mystics and saints may also point the way to how to pray in adoration.

Praise, on the other hand, is quite familiar to us. In its simplest form, it is a compliment. We know (or should know) how to tell someone that he or she has done a good job, looks wonderful, created a beautiful piece of art or made us happy.

Similarly, we "compliment" God for the magnificence, mystery and beauty of all Divinity's creations, for our joyful sense of the Spirit moving within us, for the miracle of life—and the miracle of prayer. In our prayers of praise, however, we raise the art of compliment to its highest pinnacle—wholehearted glory, awe and wonder. With passion, with happiness and with humility, we praise the Divine's never-ending bounty.

Prayer of Praise

Oh Thou that stayst the earth and hast Thy
firm throne thereon, whoso'er Thou art,

unfathomable to human knowledge, whether
thou art Zeus or the necessity of Nature,
or the mind of man, to Thee I raise my voice.

EURIPIDES

To stand on one leg and prove God's existence is a very different thing
from going down on one's knees and thanking him.

SØREN KIERKEGAARD

Thanksgiving

All that we receive from the Divine—in the relationship of prayer, in the world around us, in the simple weave of our days and nights—are freely given and unmerited gifts of love, grace and healing. Every day we must look for ways to honor the Divine's limitless magnanimity with our prayers of thanksgiving. Open, sincere and unconditional gratitude for the Divine's blessings further sanctifies our relationship with God in prayer and moves us to approach the world outside prayer with the same attitude of sincere gratefulness.

In the morning we can thank God for arriving whole and refreshed to start a new day. In the evening we can give thanks for that same day well spent and its small blessings: work done well, children home safe, food on the table, the love of friends and family. We also offer prayers of thanksgiving for larger gifts and blessings: a healed body or soul, a lost child returned home, a catastrophe avoided, a broken relationship made whole, a war ended, a healthy newborn arrived safe and sound.

We may also practice what some spiritual teachers call

the prayer of "vicarious" thanksgiving, offering God prayers of gratitude for the blessings and gifts, large and small, that other individuals are given but that are taken for granted and never acknowledged.

Indeed, as we mature in our prayer lives with the Divine, we will discover that we spend less time praying about self and our personal needs and more time offering prayers of thanksgiving. As our hearts open ever wider and our spirits become more infused with the awesome presence of the Divine, we will find more things about which to be grateful every day, even including—and perhaps especially including—the hardships, trials and setbacks we inevitably endure but from which we gain renewed faith in and reliance on God and ourselves.

Prayer of Thanksgiving

Most gracious God, by whose knowledge the depths are broken up,
and the clouds drop down the dew; We yield Thee
unfeigned thanks and praise for the return of seed-time and harvest,
for the increase of the ground and the gathering in of the fruits
thereof, and for all other blessings of thy merciful providence
bestowed upon this nation and people. . . .

THE BOOK OF COMMON PRAYER

Create in me a clean heart, O God.

PSALM 51:10

Contrition

The concept of sin is a very unpopular one these days. In fact, if we are to believe what we read and hear and see, it seems that no one is consciously guilty of doing anything wrong anymore. We have become a nation of blamers and a people of excuses, justifications and rationalizations. We rarely accept responsibility for our less-than-exemplary behavior, but we are marvelously adept at pointing the finger at those who "make us" do what we do: our mothers, our fathers, our government, our society, our priests, our rabbis, our schools.

Honorable and decent behavior, certainly at the public level, seems a mostly absent thing. We should be outraged that even our most trusted public servants can't behave better than feral ten-year-olds. Instead, we snicker and giggle behind our hands at their antics.

Oh yes, sin we do—call it what we may. After all these years, and after all the heartbreak and social calls to arms—and despite the fact that surely we should know better by now—our world is still gutted with racism and bigotry, war, child abuse, institutionalized poverty and homelessness, large-scale pollution, corporate deceit. And those are just the big-ticket items in the sin bazaar.

What of our less dramatic and less public failings? What about our lack of compassion for those who are different than we, who have less money and power, less knowledge and social cachet? What about our rampant self-absorption and urge to acquire more money, more things, more space, more power? What about our anger, our selfishness, our small-mindedness?

When we juxtapose the baseness of even our smallest sins against the unconditional, unmerited love and grace we are freely offered by the Divine, we see the need for regular prayers of contrition or confession. At least once a week we should do a thorough self-inventory of our sins, failings and falls from grace with our families and friends, in the community, at work or at play. We should then lay out our transgressions, large and small, before the Divine on the altar of contrition. We pray not only for God's forgiveness, but for the strength and courage to change our old habits and behaviors and transform our relationship with the world. If we have hurt others, intentionally or not, we also pray for the humility to ask for forgiveness from them.

Prayers of contrition are of inestimable value to both our private prayer lives and our public selves. Contrition sweeps away the musty and tainted detritus of human living that we too often drag into our relationship with God in prayer, and that prevents us from growing in faith and love. With contrition, we are forgiven, restored, renewed. Because we are forgiven in prayer by the Divine, we are ourselves empowered to forgive others who have hurt us.

Prayer of Contrition

My patient God, forgive!
Praying Thy pardon sweet
I lay a lonely heart
Before Thy feet.

ETHAN CARBERRY

Spread out your petition before God, and then say, "Thy will,
not mine, be done." The sweetest lesson I have learned in
God's school is to let the Lord choose for me.

Dwight L. Moody

Petition

When we offer prayers of petition or supplication, we
bring to God any and all of our unique needs, concerns
and special requests, however big or small. We may pray
for healing, for relief from anger or pain, for the restoration
of a broken relationship, for new knowledge and grace
with which to move in the world, for help in getting a job
done or dealing with a difficult person.

Even though the Divine is an "anticipatory" God who
knows what we need—and what we will ask for—before
we do, asking God for help within the intimacy of the
prayer relationship is an act of faith and humility. Through
our prayers of petition we demonstrate our humble belief
that we can do nothing and can accomplish nothing in the
world alone and through our own devices. We need to feel
the Divine's hand gently pushing us forward, molding us
into the people we were meant to be.

Prayers of petition, however passionate and plaintive, do
not guarantee that we will get what we are asking for, and
we must be prepared for that eventuality. Not getting what
we pray for doesn't mean we haven't been heard,
or haven't prayed well, or aren't worthy. Not getting what
we pray for simply means that for today, our petition
is not the Divine's will for us. Prayers of petition, then, also
become acts of trust for us, where we learn to acknowledge

that not only does God know what we need before we even ask, but God also knows what's best for us, and what's best for us is not always the thing we desire most.

Prayer of Petition

O Lord my God, I have trusted in thee;
O Jesus my dearest one, now set me free.
In prison's oppression, in sorrow's obsession,
I weary for thee.
With sighing and crying bowed down as dying,
I adore thee, I implore thee, set me free!

MARY, QUEEN OF SCOTS

There is nothing that makes us love a man
so much as praying for him.

WILLIAM LAW

Intercession

When we offer prayers of intercession, we pray for the needs and concerns of other people, both those we know intimately and those we know not at all. Like prayers of petition, intercessory prayers may cover a range of needs and concerns, both large and small. We may pray for comfort and healing for someone who has been diagnosed with an illness or who has lost a spouse or child. We may also offer intercessory prayers for strength, courage and eventual success for those who are looking for work, or love, or who are struggling with financial problems. In fact, many people keep an ongoing intercessory prayer list to which they periodically add the names of those who need or ask for prayer.

Our prayers of intercession also extend to all of humankind. We pray for the victims of war and hunger, of random violence and abuse, of bigotry and indifference. We may even join one of the many national or international intercessory prayer groups that collectively pray for others at specific times and places.

Intercessory prayers are profoundly powerful, their compassionate words carrying the potential for great healing and renewal for all people, one person at a time. Prayers of intercession solidify our absolute connection to God together with our human connection to one another. When we offer prayers of intercession we are also reminded that not only are we wholly dependent on the Divine for comfort and sustenance, but we are wholly responsible for the comfort and sustenance of the people we share this world with.

Prayer of Intercession

Almighty God . . . Who lovest all and
forgettest none, we bring to Thee our
supplications for all Thy creatures and all
Thy children. . . . We remember before Thee
all on whom Thou hast laid the cross of suffering,
the sick in body and the weak in mind. . . . All
who have been bereaved of relations or friends
. . . all who have met with worldly loss, that in
the dark and cloudy day they may find assurance
and peace in Thee. . . .

J. Hunter

Keep us, Lord, so awake in the duties of our
calling that we may sleep in Thy peace and
wake in Thy glory.

JOHN DONNE

Oblation

When we offer prayers of oblation to the Divine—that is, words or thoughts that convey feelings such as, "Do with me what You will" or "Thy will, not mine, be done"—we offer up our very selves as tools of God, to be used in any way the Divine sees fit.

Even more, we offer ourselves as emissaries of the Divine in the physical world. As oblates, we are willing to carry God's love and spirit from the private realm of prayer and the security of our uniquely personal relationship with the Divinity into the more turbulent waters of work, family, friendship and community. Oblation implies much more than just a "missionary" or "evangelical" instinct. Offers of oblation must be accompanied by great humility, coupled with a deep commitment to share God's love with all of humankind. We may do this in prayer, in actions, through our work or our art, and especially through our relationships with others.

Prayers of oblation also imply that we are willing to take up whatever mantle God throws us and go whatever distance is required. We can only do that if we have a deep relationship with the Divine, a strong sense of ourselves, a steadfast faith, a healthy ego, and unconditional love and compassion for our human family. Christ was a singular oblate. So, too, are Buddhist bodhisattvas, spiritual masters guided by wisdom and compassion, who put aside their own ultimate enlightenment to teach others the way to Buddhahood.

If we are sincere and patient through our prayers of oblation, in time the Divine will reveal to us what path we should take to be an emissary of God's love. Each oblate's path will be unique to him or her, but all oblates are united by their love and concern for others, and by their willingness to put the needs of others before their own.

Prayer of Oblation

Lead me, O God, and Thou my destiny,
To that one place which You will have me fill:
I follow gladly. Should I strive with Thee
A recreant, I needs must follow still.

CLEANTHES
GREEK STOIC, 3RD CENTURY B.C.

The mystery and rewards of prayer are limitless, and we can only scratch the surface here. You will discover for yourself the profound gifts and insights of this singularly interior spiritual journey when you begin to practice prayer regularly, one day at a time. To do that, you need to know how to begin to prepare yourself, physically and mentally, for the process of prayer. We discuss that fully in chapter 4.

But before we begin even to prepare for prayer, we need to take a deeper look at why people pray and what benefits they derive from prayer.

3

Why Pray?

*Prayer is a kind of calling home every day. And there can come
to you a serenity, a feeling of at-homeness in God's universe, a peace
that the world can neither give nor disturb, a fresh courage,
a new insight, a holy boldness, that you'll never, never get any
other way.*

EARL G. HUNT JR.

THE GIFTS OF PRAYER: WHY WE PRAY

The habitual practice of prayer, especially daily prayer, will yield profound gifts over time. Through the ages, all great spiritual masters, saints and teachers, as well as practitioners of every spiritual tradition, have told us that the blessed bounties of prayer are both inestimable and limitless.

No doubt some of us come to prayer looking for the same gifts that mystics and theologians have described in sacred texts for centuries. Most of these gifts—the reasons that we pray—fall in the realm of deepening our relationship with the Divine, undergoing spiritual, mental and emotional transformations, and developing new views of and relationships with the world and its people.

In modern times, some religious leaders and lay people have ascribed to the practice of prayer even more sophisticated, contemporary and materialistic benefits—some real and meaningful, some capricious and false. Prayer is said to be the pathway to everything from instant healing to success in love, from financial windfalls to accelerated plant growth, from raised serotonin levels (the "feel good" chemicals of the brain) to better recovery rates from heart attacks, from improved performances at work and sports to mystical communion with angels and demons.

It is impossible to list all the reasons that people pray. The reasons are as different as the people doing the praying.

And as each one of us has a very particular and individual relationship with God, so, too, are the benefits of prayer subtly different from person to person. Finally, what we want and expect to get from prayer as unique individuals with one-of-a-kind relationships with the Divine are as various as the stars in the sky.

Still, spiritual teachers throughout time have consistently celebrated several benefits of prayer that are common to all who pray honestly and regularly.

All these gifts do not drop into our laps at once, of course, but are gradually revealed and made manifest as our relationship with God in prayer deepens. Still, some gifts are bestowed at the moment we begin to pray, beginning with our first "yes" to the Divine.

*All who have walked with God have viewed
prayer as the main business of their lives.*

DELMA JACKSON

Our "Yes" to the Divine
Opens a Portal to Our Souls

We know now that the impulse to pray comes directly from the Divine as an unmerited gift, freely given. Prayer as gift is an expression of God's unconditional love for us. When we follow the impulse to pray, we are led into an exclusive and mutual love relationship with the Divine in prayer.

Our resounding "yes" to this call to relationship through prayer with the Divine is also the first gift of prayer. This "yes" to God is like no other "yes" in our lives. It is a "yes" of sweet, deep and faith-filled surrender, a "yes" of humility, a "yes" of yearning and a "yes" of acknowledgment. We need something greater than ourselves in our lives, if only as example, if we are to mature spiritually into the children of God we were meant to be and the compassionate people the world needs.

The faith implicit in the "yes" of surrender, together with the humility, yearning and firm belief in something infinitely loving who exists both outside of us and within us, are the recurrent themes and challenges of a life of prayer. They appear again and again in the course of our prayer lives as motifs of our spiritual journey. They melodiously sound the depths of our inner explorations in prayer, as we go deeper and deeper to meet the Divine in relationship, and as we peel away the detritus of our own willfulness, false selves and human shortcomings.

The "yes" of sweet and deep surrender that is our first act of faith on entering prayer is also a gift of freedom— freedom from our self-centeredness and self-seeking and the loneliness that attends them. We say "yes" to the invitation to something wholly unknown in which we surrender, little by little, our dancing egos and frenetic self-wills. This "yes" to the plunge into the unknown of prayer says we are willing, finally, to give up the reins of ego-driven control and begin to trust that if we take the leap into prayer, we will be caught and held in the arms of our God. There we will learn to understand and embrace the Divine's will for us, a heavenly thread that weaves through our lives from their beginnings to their ends. Embracing God's will for us will ultimately deliver the gifts of deep happiness and enduring inner peace that we all seek.

Surrendering the false self is wonderfully freeing—we are no longer alone in the mystery, magic and misery of being human. Someone else holds the master plans of our lives, and those plans are wholly good and grace-filled. This Great Someone is ever guiding our lives and will never abandon us, no matter how many false turns and missteps we take along the spiritual path. God is always present within our hearts as long as we keep returning to prayer and saying "yes, yes, yes!"

The purpose of prayer is to reveal the presence
of God equally present, all the time, in every condition.

OSWALD CHAMBERS

We Experience an Ever-Deepening Awareness of God

As we return to prayer again and again in surrender, faith, humility and trust, as we listen ever more attentively for the voice of the Divine, we come to understand how very real God's presence is: within us, within everyone around us, within everything that encompasses our world.

This is without a doubt the greatest gift of prayer: to become gradually aware, and then to know absolutely that there is a Divine Power, and that that Divinity is alive and a part of us always. The inexplicable and indefinable presence of God within and without variously awes, astonishes and humbles us when first we begin to glimpse God's presence in prayer. Very soon, however, we joyfully anticipate the approach of God's presence, accompanied as it is by such encompassing love, compassion, forgiveness and understanding.

As we return to prayer day after day, our awareness of God increases proportionately, and soon the early glimmers of a Divine presence become a constant and warming light ever at the center of our beings. It is impossible to explain what the presence of God feels like in the heart and spirit, but it is palpable and enduring—and one of the earliest gifts of prayer.

Every time you pray, if your prayer is
sincere, there will be new feeling and new
meaning in it which will give you fresh
courage, and you will understand that prayer
is an education.

FYODOR DOSTOEVSKY

We Come to Understand and Embrace Our Authentic Selves

With our new awareness of the Divine's presence within us and around us also comes the knowledge of our own Divinity. As we said in the beginning of this book, in this extraordinary journey home to the Divine through prayer, we are not simply human beings trying to be spiritual. We have always *been* spiritual beings, breathed into existence by the fiery love of the Ultimate Divinity, but often burdened by the heavy mantle of our temporary humanity.

Too soon, as time goes by, we forget what we knew instinctively as children—that we both come from the

Divine and are partly Divine ourselves. As God carries us into and through life, we carry God within our hearts—to our work, our play, our family, our friends.

Prayer gently reintroduces us to the part of our selves that is wholly Divine. And having looked in the mirror of prayer and seen in our own faces the image of God, we cannot go back to being the Spirit-less beings we were before prayer.

We are, therefore, led by prayer to reexamine who we have been, who we are now, and who we can be for God and for others in the world.

Have ego and self-seeking been the driving energies in our lives? Does our work reflect who we really are and how we want to be in the world? Are our relationships with others open and meaningful, imbued with grace, respect and tolerance? Or are our relationships shallow, spiteful, short-lived? What do we do to make a difference in the world and for the people around us? Are we quick to love, forgive, empathize, show compassion?

These are some of the questions we ask ourselves in prayer as we begin the critical work of dismantling our old, self-seeking selves, layer by layer by layer, until we fully uncover the Divinity at our core. This is hard and sometimes painful work, but it is also joyous work. How glorious to know who we really are and what we are capable of being—which is anything and everything! How extraordinary to know we are never alone. How wondrous to put on again the holy vestments of our reborn, God-filled selves and step out into the world transformed, to embrace, love and serve.

Prayer opens our eyes so that we may see
ourselves and others as God sees us.

CLARA PALMER

As We Understand Ourselves Better, So We Understand Others Better

When we "return" to the world from the relationship of prayer as remade spirits—sanctified, renewed, wrapped in Divine love and compassion, and thoroughly in touch with the God at our centers—we cannot help but look at and feel differently about the people with whom we share our world.

Knowing now that we are Divine children of God, we recognize the same Divinity in those around us. We are indeed sisters and brothers in a world that should have no boundaries. And as we have been embraced so profoundly in prayer by God, been bathed in the Divine Light of unconditional love, compassion and forgiveness, so we ourselves try to be more loving, compassionate and forgiving in our relationships with our Divine extended family.

We too try to become beacons of Divine Light in all our dealings with people. In prayer we have done the hard work of searching our souls and stripping away the base, banal and mean-spirited parts of ourselves. We understand why we were the people we used to be, doing the things we felt we had to do. And as we have come to understand and forgive ourselves, we can't help but extend our understanding and forgiveness to all those we encounter.

If resentment, anger and bitterness framed many of our relationships, we often discover, sometimes with astonishment, that those negative feelings have disappeared. Our relationships are now colored by a new tolerance and openness, a willingness to live and let live, a genuine happiness and enthusiasm for others' good fortune. We become quick to love, to forgive and to forget. We are less inclined to be suspicious, angry, solitary. We genuinely seek out and enjoy the company of others, not for what they can give us or do for us, but for what we all share in common—the kiss of the Divine, the imprint of God on our souls, the voice of God in our hearts.

What an extraordinary world indeed it would be if we experienced in our very marrow the presence of God in everyone we met. Prayer takes us leap years toward that ultimate experience.

Prayer is the spirit speaking truth to Truth.

PHILIP JAMES BAILEY

Our Reverence for All Things Deepens

We not only care deeply about others, we care deeply about the world we all share. It is no coincidence that in the last twenty-five years or so, as people have been searching for new spiritual meaning in their lives, there has been a parallel concern about preserving the earth, its animals, the land, the sky, the waters.

When we were breathed into being by the Divine, we were breathed into a world already fully formed and glorious in all its aspects. Laid out before us was every imaginable creature . . . every tree, leaf, flower and rock . . . every mountain and ocean . . . sunsets, sunrises, rainbows . . . wind and rain and heat and snow . . . stars and planets . . . every color, sound and texture we could dream about or hope for. As children of the Divine in this world, we were meant to be caretakers of all this Divine bounty, all this glory. We bungled the job mightily.

In prayer, however, we not only experience the Divine in ourselves and in others, but we come to understand that Divinity is present in everything in creation. We come to honor and respect our obligation to care for the world as the sacred trust that it is. Prayer gives us the gift of new eyes as we look out at creation, and encourages us to reassume the role of its concerned and loving caretakers.

Only in prayer do we achieve that complete
and harmonious assembly of body, mind and
spirit which gives the frail human reed its
unshakable strength.

ALEXIS CARREL

We Are Healed: Spiritually, Emotionally and Psychologically

If we stay the course with prayer, through dry and dark and empty times when we cannot feel the presence of the Divine, and no one answers when we call out from our loneliness and fear (and this will happen; it is a test of our love and faith), there will be a moment, a day, a night when we break through to a new level of prayer and an awareness of God that is utterly ineffable and exquisitely sweet.

We will feel those parts of ourselves that are still broken, tender and aching, and that have been set adrift in our souls for so long, come together again with a gentle whoosh . . . and we will be gloriously whole, forever convinced of our own Divinity, maddeningly aware of God in everything around us, always calling to us joyfully, invitingly.

We will laugh as we never have before—prayerful people are joyous people—because we will sense the sacred silliness in all we experience, touch, do and think. We will never take ourselves too seriously again; we have found our special place in the Divine's plan and we are happily secure there, knowing all is well and all is good.

We will also experience profound wonder and love, awe and inspiration. Anger will go. Depression will lift. We will never be lonely again. Love will drive all we say and do.

Our prayers will become mostly prayers of adoration and praise and thanksgiving. We will ask for little now, because we know we have been given all we will ever need. We will move easily, back and forth, from verbal prayer to contemplative prayer.

And in one very special moment in time—and this is rare, but it happens—we will be held transfixed and immovable in the presence of the Divine. We will no longer be praying; someone else will take over. We will become prayer itself. We will become God's prayer.

Prayer has marked the trees across the
wilderness of a skeptical world to direct
the traveler in distress.

DOUGLAS MEADER

We Are Called Through Prayer to Be God's Emissaries in the World

All the gifts of prayer will be rendered hollow and meaningless if we do not share them with our sisters and brothers, if we do not carry them with us into the world.

Most people who make a sacred commitment to a relationship with the Divine in prayer, and who practice prayer daily, are eventually drawn to some sort of service in the world, where they can be that "single light" of God's love, compassion, joy and understanding for others.

Most of us cannot lead the kind of life that a Mother Teresa did, and most of us don't want to evangelize either. Few of us are called to those kinds of service anyway.

But many of us can do volunteer work that emulates the Divine's unconditional love and compassion. And all of us can make a conscious decision to honor the Divinity in ourselves and in others by infusing our daily lives, including and especially our work, with the many other gifts that we have received from God in prayer: empathy, forgiveness, patience, faithfulness, tenderness, concern and selflessness, to name just a few. How extraordinarily rich our relationships would be if we could bring just a portion of such gifts to just a part of our daily lives.

And these are only some of the gifts of prayer. Many of prayer's gifts are so intimate, so uniquely personal, that we cannot—and wouldn't want to—put a name to them. These special gifts are private and sacred convenants with the Divine. These are the gifts we are allowed to keep just for ourselves, to hold closely to our hearts, to cherish in our most private and holy moments.

They are there, simply for the taking, when we return God's call to prayer with a "yes" in our hearts and a commitment of body and soul.

How we finally pray when we have said "yes" and committed body and soul is the subject of chapter 5.

The very best and utmost of attainment in
this life is to remain still and let God
act and speak in thee.

MEISTER ECKHART

4

Where Do We Begin?

I have to hurry all day to make time to pray.

MARTIN LUTHER

PREPARING FOR PRAYER

In the best of all possible worlds, our lives would be orderly and sane. There would be time enough in each of our days to do all the things we need and want to do, and we would do them with ease and grace. Our priorities would be straight, our days and nights would be our own. And prayer, a basically simple and organic process, would be as fundamental a part of our daily agendas as waking and sleeping, commuting to work, bathing our children, walking our dogs, cooking our meals and mowing our lawns. Somewhere in the midst of our very full lives, praying would have its own sanctified place.

But that would be in the best of worlds. Instead, our days are rarely orderly and sane. There is never enough time to do what we need to do, let alone what we want to do. Establishing priorities has become a cosmic juggling act. We cheat on sleep, awaken groggy, grab a café au lait to go, dash to our trains, skip baths in favor of showers, hire dogwalkers, order take-out and let the grass grow until our neighbors scream.

If our feet barely ever touch the ground, how in heaven will we find the time and place to fall to our knees? As with many things, preparation is the key.

My words fly up, my thoughts remain below:
Words without thoughts never to heaven go.

SHAKESPEARE'S HAMLET

Adding something new to our crowded schedules is a daunting prospect, no matter how good it feels and how good it may be for us. Deciding to add prayer to our lives is not unlike deciding to shut off the television and start exercising regularly. Cultivating a life of prayer is like cultivating any new and healthful habit. We may have to shed some old habits along the way, and that prospect can be frightening or unsettling at the start. All good habits take work and time. And work is what we have too much of, time too little. How do we begin to prepare to pray?

For many, the journey to prayer first begins in the heart as a gentle yearning. And for a long time it may remain only a yearning—we simply have the intention to pray. We want to make prayer a part of the web of our lives, but we're not sure why and we're not sure how. We have already talked much about yearning and about the what and why of prayer in chapters 2 and 3.

Finding a Place for Prayer

When we decide that yearning isn't enough and action is called for, we begin trying to find some room for prayer in our lives. We take a hard look at our agendas and begin to clear out some space for prayer. What things must stay, what things can go, where can we cut back to make room for prayer? We carve out a new space in our time—however small—and it becomes our inviolable place for prayer.

Finally, when we find a place for prayer, we come to that place well prepared. Any new habit requires more than yearning and good intentions. Desire may get us to our knees, but it won't keep us there. Good habits flourish with the more time, attention and planning that we give them. Cultivating a prayerful life is no different.

When we have a firm notion of how, what and when we will pray, we don't have to rely on inspiration for results. With a structure in which to pray, our initial yearnings translate to action, and action brings results.

This chapter is about actively preparing for prayer, about building a framework in which to pray on a regular basis, so that over time prayer comes as naturally to us as breathing. All spiritual seekers—from Benedictine contemplatives to Buddhist monks, Sufi dervishes to Orthodox rabbis, devotees of Gaia to celebrants of the Mother Goddess—understand the spiritual benefits of having a specific time and place for prayer and a set of rituals and practices that root them in that time and place.

We prepare for prayer in two ways: externally and internally. External preparation involves finding the right physical environment in which to pray. It is about finding a prayerful corner to which in time we faithfully bring our physical selves. Internal preparation for prayer involves creating the right interior environment for prayer. It is about nurturing the mind and heart in soulful ways that anchor the body in the act of prayer.

Prayer time must be kept up as duly as meal-time.

MATTHEW HENRY

SETTING THE SCENE: EXTERNAL PREPARATION

When we externally prepare for prayer, we need to consider five essential factors: when we will pray; where we will pray; how we will minimize distractions and interruptions; how much time we will devote to each prayer session; and what rituals or actions, physical postures or gestures, will support the act of praying.

When Will We Pray?

For ordinary folk who do not live in monasteries, temples or mosques, and who must cope with the demands of family and work, carving out some precious time to pray can be a challenge. But establishing a reasonable prayer schedule—one we can stick to—is crucial to cultivating the good habit of prayer. So we first need to decide how much time we can give to prayer. Will we pray daily, weekly or only during special holy days, feasts and retreats? The important thing here is to find a comfortable, comforting and manageable time for prayer in our lives, and then keep returning to it again and again.

Daily Prayer

Almost all spiritual disciplines celebrate daily prayer as the ideal, and for many people, early morning prayer is the logical place to start. Ten minutes in thoughtful contemplation before rising from bed, or twenty minutes in devotional prayer at the kitchen table, clears the emotional decks, helps establish priorities and sets a spiritual rhythm to our day.

When the demands of getting to work on time—or making lunches and putting the children on the school bus—make early morning prayer difficult, we may need to get creative about finding a space for daily prayer. Time spent commuting is also an excellent time for silent prayer or devotional reading. Or, when we arrive at our offices, we can shut the door for ten minutes, close our eyes and offer up our work as prayer.

Other people postpone prayer until the noon hour. Then they may devote part of their lunch hour to meditative prayer, or spend twenty minutes in contemplation in a nearby chapel, park or public garden. In Old World Christian countries, noon was the classic time to pray the Angelus, a prayer of adoration in celebration of the Incarnation of Christ. The Angelus bells would ring at noon across towns and cities. People would stop whatever they were doing, stand, turn to the sound of the bells and observe a minute of silent prayer. Whatever our beliefs, we, too, can use the noon hour to create our own Angelus prayer, a moment of silent adoration to a power or spirit greater than ourselves.

Still other people use mealtime—and especially dinnertime—as an occasion for daily prayer. Drawing from the rich abundance of mealtime grace prayers available, and on the power of the family united around the table to break bread, we may offer up our prayers not only in gratitude for the food before us, but for all the blessings of the day.

For many other people, evening, particularly late evening, is a rich time—and often the only time—for private and deeply personal prayer. Late evening is often the easiest time to find twenty or thirty extra minutes, sometimes right before sleep, when the world around us has finally settled down and all is quiet and expectant. Evening is a marvelous time for petitional prayer or for rapt adoration.

Weekly Prayer

Adding daily prayer to our schedules may be impossible or too intimidating when we first begin to cultivate the habit of prayer. Instead, many people center their prayer life around a weekly ritual, holy day or Sabbath celebration.

One weekly ritual that many people are exploring is the self-structured mini-retreat. Every weekend, two or three hours are set aside solely for the purpose of spiritual sustenance and renewal. Some people take themselves out into nature to retreat, drawing inspiration from the natural world around them. Others retreat to their bedrooms or back yards, shutting off the phone and letting their family know that they are not to be disturbed.

Mini-retreats require planning, preparation and self-discipline, but they are wonderful opportunities to nurture the soul and explore a variety of prayer techniques: mindfulness meditation; contemplative or reflective prayer; verbal and silent prayers of adoration, praise, thanksgiving or petition; spiritual journaling; and physical movement as prayer. The spiritual nourishment and awareness garnered in such retreats then sustain us through the new week to come.

Other people center their weekly prayer within the traditional Sabbath liturgies of their church, temple, mosque or synagogue. There they are both inspired and comforted by the familiar rituals and prayers, and they are buoyed by the power of community. Group prayer, centered around commonly shared beliefs and traditions, is a powerful experience that may also sustain us from week to week and inspire us to explore new and solitary paths of prayer.

Annual or Occasional Prayer

Finally, some people center their prayer lives around annual feasts or events, pilgrimages or retreats. For many of these people, daily prayer or meditation is already an indispensable part of their lives, but it is frequently non-denominational, quiet and private, unattached to traditional rituals and liturgies. For these people, annual feasts, pilgrimages and retreats become an opportunity for mindful—and specifically, prayerful—self-reflection and life review, a time to take an inventory of where one has been over the last year and where one wants to go in the future.

On the altar in my hermitage in France are images
of Buddha and Jesus, and every time I light incense, I touch both of
them as my spiritual ancestors.

THICH NHAT HANH

Where Will We Pray?

Some people can pray anywhere: they close their eyes, open their hearts, shut out the world and just do it. But most of us need a private and quiet place in which to pray. Even beloved Buddhist master Thich Nhat Hanh—hailed because his very life is a prayer—still sets aside a corner of his room for special morning and evening devotions.

Unless we are among the very few and blessed people who can set aside a separate room in our homes as a private prayer chapel, sometimes a "corner" of a room is all the place we have—or need—to pray. Many people set up a special spot in their bedrooms for prayer, perhaps putting a table and chair there, a prie–dieu, or a meditation cushion.

Other people are most comfortable doing their praying in a quiet, darkened and nearly empty church or temple, mosque or synagogue, surrounded by familiar and tradition–laden religious icons. Still others draw their greatest spiritual inspiration from nature. They are most comfortable praying under the majesty of the night sky, or in tandem with the gentle rhythms of the ocean, or amidst the rich sights and sounds of the forest.

Many other people use the time that they commute to work for praying. Choosing a window seat in the back row of a bus or train can provide an almost private sanctuary for personal prayer time.

When prayer is a struggle, do not worry about the prayers that you cannot pray. You yourself are a prayer. . . .

O. HALLESBY

How Do We Minimize Distractions and Interruptions?

We can take some simple precautions to preserve the sanctity and privacy of our prayer time. If we are praying at home, we can disconnect the phone for a half hour, ask other family members not to disturb us, and shut the door to our prayer space. If we have chosen a commuter train or bus as our prayer place, we can use a Walkman and earphones to play some gentle meditative music as background. And if nature is our sacred place, we would do well to choose a spot along the ocean or in the woods that is neither too deserted nor too overrun with tourists. Here, both safety and sanctuary are important.

Short prayers pierceth Heaven.

THE CLOUD OF UNKNOWING

How Long Will We Pray?

Ideally we should pray as long as we are comfortable with praying. But it is not so much time as it is preparation and intention that make for successful prayer. Indeed, locking ourselves into too long and rigid a prayer posture will often sabotage our good intentions—a fact that many beginning meditators painfully discover as they find themselves focusing more on the aches in their knees than on the rapture in their hearts.

Certainly we need to give prayer a chance to "take" hold. And that means not only allowing enough time for prayer itself, but also allowing enough time to prepare for prayer—time to settle into our place of prayer, to relax our bodies and quiet our minds, to light a candle, perhaps, or some incense and then take a moment or two to fix our prayer intention firmly in our hearts.

Start with allowing yourself twenty to thirty minutes for prayer, about half of which will be time just to settle into your prayer space and prayerful state, take several deep, cleansing breaths, relax your body, quiet your mind and focus on the presence of the Divine.

Prayerful Rituals, Postures and Gestures

We can add much to the richness and texture of our prayers by borrowing one or more of the classic rituals, postures and gestures of prayer. These are physical cues that alert the body, mind and heart to the fact that we are about to do something different and very special: We are about to pray.

Physical cues also help relax the body and focus the mind more quickly, so we can settle into prayer faster and more easily. There are as many sacred rituals, postures and gestures as there are ways to pray. Here are just a few of them.

Rituals

Before we go to our place of prayer, we may first want to wash our hands as a gesture of benediction and humility. As we hold our hands under the running water, we wash away the day's accumulations of petty hurts, resentments and improprieties, and we come to prayer refreshed and empty-handed, ready for anything. When we enter our prayer place, we may then wish to light a candle and perhaps a stick of incense, to honor the sacredness of this special time. And if we have also created a small altar in our prayer place, for sacred images or objects, we may want to bow to that altar, as a gesture of respect, before we assume a posture for prayer.

Prayer moves the hand that moves the world.

JOHN AIKMAN WALLACE

Postures

There are many postures for prayer, and some postures lend themselves more readily to certain kinds of prayer. Prayers of petition and contrition seem more naturally done on one's knees. Contemplative prayer and prayers of adoration and thanksgiving are often more comfortably done while seated. Reflective or meditative prayer is frequently done while seated or walking. Try different prayer postures at different times and note how and if the quality of your prayer or your attention changes. But do remember that remaining comfortable and focused while praying is always the primary consideration. In the end, there is no wrong way to pray. You may pray on your knees or on your feet—standing, walking or whirling. You may pray seated on a meditation cushion, a blanket or a chair. You may even pray prostrate on your chest or flat on your back. Simply find the most comfortable way to pray, one that allows you to stay focused, relaxed and respectful.

Gestures

Where and how we use our hands during prayer can also help prepare us to pray, quickly focusing our attention and lending a deep resonance to the quality of our prayer. Here, as with posture, we have many traditions from which to borrow sacred and anchoring gestures. Here are two.

When we pray—whether sitting, kneeling, standing or walking—we may join the palms of our hands together, fingers pointed to the sky in classic "steeple" fashion. Then, with head slightly bowed, we either hold our joined hands to our chest, in the Western tradition, or to our forehead, in the Eastern tradition. Both gestures are so universal, so ancient and so purely sacred in origin that they reside like trace memories in our bodies, absolute cues that we are about to do something special, something beyond the common and everyday. Experiment with one of these gestures now. Take a moment, bow your head, join your hands and hold them to your chest or forehead. Take a breath . . . can you feel it? The body quiets; it knows something's up.

In seated prayer, particularly contemplative and reflective prayer, we may borrow another classic gesture from the East. Our hands rest open, palms up and slightly cupped, one on each thigh. The index and thumb on each hand are touching slightly, forming a closed circle. This classic praying posture has three benefits: our chest, and therefore our heart, is unobstructed and open to the prayer experience; our hands, too, are open and receptive, waiting to receive whatever prayer has to offer; the closed circles our fingers form serve both to ground and contain our innate spiritual energy, keeping it within us. This is the energy that is called *qi, chi* and *prana* in the East; soul or spirit in the West. When we pray in this way, we are joined to a multitude of traditions and ancestors on both sides of the world whose origins go back almost six thousand years.

When you begin to cultivate the habit of prayer, experiment with time and place, posture and gesture. In that way you will find your own unique rhythm and beat for prayer, one that will sustain you for years to come.

Prayer at its best is the expression of the total life, for all things else being equal, our prayers are only as powerful as our lives.

A. W. TOZER

MIND OVER MATTER: INTERNAL ATTITUDE

All the sacred gestures and postures in the world, all the prayerful spaces and borrowed time, will come to naught if we bring to prayer an empty heart or agitated mind. When we come to prayer from a broken place, it is often hard to put a voice to prayer.

Or we may be going happily along, cultivating our new habit of prayer, and then suddenly hit a long, dry, white season where we come to our prayer spaces spiritually empty, time and time again.

Sometimes we may have our exterior landscape of prayer in place, but our interior landscape is temporarily barren.

Preparing internally for prayer involves learning how to use simple aids that buffet the act of prayer and understanding how to practice the art of "collecting oneself" through simple spiritual exercises.

Aids to Prayer

The most common aids for praying utilize touch, sight, sound and breath as grounding rods.

Touch

For many people, prayer ropes (*malas*), beads and rosaries are invaluable aids to prayer, particularly when we find it hard to pray contemplatively or reflectively. Fingering the knots and beads of ropes and rosaries, we can recite simple, repetitive prayers or mantras that keep us in our sacred spaces for a time, and eventually act to open our hearts and minds again to larger prayer. For other people, holding a special object that has personal and sacred meaning to them—a stone, a feather, a piece of sea glass, a small cross or icon, to name just a few examples—while they offer up their prayers also is a fine grounding device.

Sight

For others of us, visually focusing on a sacred object— a cross, candle or icon—while we pray or simply sitting with receptivity and awareness is a most powerful prayer aid. So, too, is the act of focusing on a flower blossom or an intricately worked mandala—a sacred and symbolic circular pattern used as a focus during meditation.

For still others, reading sacred or spiritual texts, or lyrical poetry—or even writing in a spiritual journal—all have an invaluable place in the life of prayer. For many, these activities become moments of prayer themselves; for still others, they are gentle preludes to prayer.

Sound

Sacred or meditative music, softly played in the background of our prayer space, can be a profoundly anchoring tool. And the timbre and rhythm of our own voices, raised in a one-word mantra of praise and adoration— *Abba, Om, Allah, Spiritus, Maranatha*—has long held a special place in the art of prayer.

Breath

For many people, particularly those who have practiced meditation, there is no finer prayer aid than the soft and simple flow of one's own breath. Practitioners of this prayer tool may focus on the sensation of their breath as it enters and leaves their nostrils. Or they may count each inhalation and exhalation, using breath to settle their spirits, focus their thoughts and practice mindfulness.

Another technique using breath and words as a focus for prayer is to choose a one- or two-sentence prayer or sacred phrase, inhaling as we slowly pray the first part or first sentence of the phrase or prayer, and exhaling as we pray the final words or phrases. Your body will quickly let you know where you should naturally inhale and exhale.

The Jesus Prayer of the Eastern Orthodox tradition is often used in this manner. One variation of that prayer, using the breath, is:

(Inhale) *Most Sacred Heart of Jesus,*
(Exhale) *have mercy on me.*
(Inhale) *Most Sacred Heart of Jesus,*
(Exhale) *hear my prayer.*

Another example of prayer-as-breath is this variation on a Buddhist prayer of loving kindness:

(Inhale) *May all of us be filled with loving kindness.*
(Exhale) *May all of us be well.*
(Inhale) *May all of us be peaceful and at ease.*
(Exhale) *May all of us be happy.*

Repeating simple phrases such as these, while slowly breathing in and out through the nose, becomes profound prayer in and of itself, and quickly quiets the minds and focuses the heart on the presence of God.

When All Is in Place: Collecting Oneself for Prayer

In collecting oneself for prayer, we use all the environmental, physical, emotional, and mental cues and actions discussed above to help quiet the mind and body, and to send a message to the spirit that prayer is about to begin.

Pay special attention to the environment in which you pray, especially if you are just beginning a life of prayer. We have already spoken about the physical space in which we pray and how to create for ourselves a prayer corner or altar.

It is worth pointing out and repeating, however, that this environment should also include silence and solitude—they are the pillars of fruitful prayer when the intention of our praying is a deeper awareness and communion with the Divine.

Of course, we can pray anywhere and imbue any environment with its own sacredness. Nature is an especially inspiring prayer space, and reflecting on the beauty and abundance of the Divine's creations can lead to rapt and heartfelt prayers of adoration and praise.

A more profound and powerful kind of prayer, however—a prayer that reaches deeply inward for the image and voice of the Divine within our own hearts, so that we may further understand God and ourselves and the relationship between us in prayer—most often occurs (and occurs most easily for many people) in a quiet place where we are alone with the Divine and self.

In that sacred, silent space and in our solitude, with all our prayer aids close at hand, we are better able to open our hearts to the voice of God, to remain focused and concentrated in our prayer, and to feel our awareness of the Divinity within and without us grow, swell and fully encompass us.

In such a sacred space, we are also better able to faith-fully practice and adhere to the four essential ingredients that we must bring to every prayer encounter with the Divine: intention, intimacy, surrender and faith. These four ingredients of prayer are the subject of our next chapter, "The Process of Prayer."

5

The Process of Prayer

When you enter your secret chamber, take plenty of time before you
begin to speak. Let quietude
wield its influence upon you. Give your soul
time to get released from the many outward things.
Give God time to play the prelude to prayer for
the benefit of your distracted soul.

O. HALLESBY

We could almost end our book here, with Hallesby's exquisite description of the prelude to and process of prayer. Hallesby, a Norwegian theologian, knew well the many forms and benefits of prayer and the depths to which our souls can be held captive by distracting, even horrific things. One of the leaders of the Nazi resistance during World War II, he survived the horrors of a German concentration camp and went on to write magnificently about prayer and the spiritual life until his death in 1961.

Hallesby is only echoing in poetic language what all the great spiritual masters through time have had to say about how to pray: find a quiet, private place for prayer; set a special time for praying; quiet your body and your mind; open yourself to the presence of the Divine; allow God to work within you. If you do just this and only this, and do it faithfully over and over, words of prayer will soon rush to your heart and then to your lips as fluidly as the waters of a natural spring. And they will be words uniquely and indelibly yours.

However, if you find it hard to just sit and wait for prayer to rise spontaneously, this book will help you find a place for and a way to prayer and relationship with the Divine.

As we bring Part One of our book to a close, then, and before you move on to use the prayers in Part Two as stepping stones along your prayer journey, it's important to review the key points about praying that we've shared in this book and offer some final thoughts for you to carry with you on the path to prayer.

We have talked about the many images of the Divine in the hopes that you will be encouraged to discover a face of God that is especially meaningful and moving to you and to you alone. Be brave about leaving behind outdated images of angry Gods and punishing Gods, exclusively male or female Gods, unapproachable, unimaginable and noninclusive Gods. Find a God that you can believe in and live with joyfully and comfortably. Listen to your heart, in the quiet of prayer, for it is there that you will find the extraordinary image of your special God.

We have also talked about how important it is to make prayer a part of your spiritual life. In fact, we believe, along with many others, that it is the most important part of your spirituality because it actively engages you in relationship with the Divine. You are moved away from obsession with self and moved forward—spiritually and emotionally—to embrace yourself and others with the same love and compassion that the Divine extends to you.

Sadly, active prayer has fallen out of favor with many people, including some theologians and religious and spiritual teachers. Verbal prayer groups that once thrived in certain religious denominations and spiritual traditions are considered passé. Prayerful action in the form of service and social justice is often celebrated over the act of prayer itself. Yet action and prayer are not mutually exclusive activities. Indeed, they are interdependent. In fact, we would go so far as to say that you cannot serve well unless you first pray well. To serve well we must understand the needs of others. We cannot understand

others' needs unless we have learned to understand ourselves. And we achieve the greatest self-understanding in
prayer, where we receive as a gift a new awareness of
both our failings and our potential glory.

We also have talked a good deal about what prayer
is and isn't, about the different ways to pray and the
different types of prayer. We have shared with you some
of the time-honored ways to create and sustain a lasting
life of prayer and facilitate the act of praying itself. We
have also looked at some of the extraordinary gifts to be
found in the relationship of prayer, the greatest of which
is the sure knowledge and awareness of the presence of
God within you, within us, within everyone and everything around us.

Our prayers must spring from the indigenous soil
of our own personal confrontation with the Spirit
of God in our lives.

MALCOLM BOYD

Moving On to Prayer: The Four Ingredients of Good Prayer

It's time to begin the journey of prayer, to move into a
dynamic relationship with the Divine, to raise our spirituality to new dimensions.

But first, a caveat and a confession: In the end, no one can
teach you how to pray. Not really. Certainly not us. Prayer
is such an individualistic and intimate act between the

knowable and the Unknowable, the seen and the Unseen, you and God, and much that will pass between you two is indefinable, indescribable—wholly none of our business. How you get to God in prayer is also a very private process and often difficult to describe, let alone teach others.

Certainly we can share with one another our own experiences with prayer and the experiences of other people who have made the journey successfully from here to There and back again through the centuries. That is what this book has been about. And we can offer as our gift to you, as we do in Part Two, some of the most beautiful, inspiring and enduring prayers that women and men have found a place for in their hearts.

At the final hour, though, you will find your way to prayer without us, in your own time and place, with your own voice and words, to discover there the meaning, mystery and majesty of your own unique God and your special relationship with that God. We urge you to do it sooner, rather than later, for the fruits of prayer are nothing less than life-sustaining.

To help you make that final leap into the arms of God, you need to bring to prayer four essential ingredients, or qualities, that spiritual writer and professor of spirituality Janet Ruffing has beautifully delineated in her article, "As Refined by Fire." Ruffing suggests that whoever we are, wherever we are, however we are feeling, and whatever our needs and wants, we must bring to prayer—along with our bodies and souls—these four things: intentionality, intimacy, surrender and fidelity.

Let's take a brief look at each of these qualities.

My prayers, my God, flow from what I am not;
I think Thy answers make me what I am.

GEORGE MacDONALD

Intentionality

Bringing intentionality to prayer simply means that we choose to pray, choose to have a relationship with the Divine in prayer, choose to make prayer a priority in our lives. Most of the time, prayer that is deep and rich and that increases our awareness of the presence of the Divine cannot be a random and spontaneous act. Instead, each and every time we pray, we must consciously choose to pray. We must say to ourselves, "This is the time and place for prayer, and I bring myself, heart and soul, to whatever prayer has to give me."

This doesn't mean that we initiate prayer. God alone calls us to the prayer relationship. Our choice is in answering "yes" or "no." And if we answer "yes," we must be prepared to open ourselves up to the experience of the Divine, to set aside our egos and self-interests, to be willing to go wherever God wants to take us in prayer. It must be our intention to do this—be open, be selfless, be willing—whenever we pray, wherever we pray.

Prayer is not eloquence, but earnestness; not
the definition of helplessness, but the feeling
of it; not figures of speech, but earnestness
of the soul.

HANNAH MORE

Intimacy

Remember that prayer is always a relationship between you and the Divine. It is a relationship that gains breadth and depth the more we pray and the more faithfully we pray. And as with all relationships, shared intimacy is an integral part of how deep and meaningful our relationship with God will become.

Intimacy renders us vulnerable and open to the Divine. We become willing to sit naked in front of God, our false selves and fabricated images tossed aside. Our true selves—fragile, frightened, timid, self-conscious, hurting, angry—are laid out at the feet of the Divine. Together, in the shared intimacy of prayer, we and God sift through the shards of our human frailties and limitations, picking them up and turning them over, holding them to the light, looking for their value, their flaws, their cracks, their soft spots. Together, we and God discover what can be discarded and what cannot. With the help of God, we eventually uncover our true selves, the inner core that is wholly Divine, the grace-filled selves that we will bring back to our families, our friends, our work, our community.

We only begin to be remade in prayer when we drop our facades and self-seeking and embrace God with utter intimacy.

O what peace we often forfeit,
O what needless pain we bear,
All because we do not carry
Everything to God in prayer!

JOSEPH SCRIVEN

Surrender

Intimacy is just one of the many acts of surrender we must bring to prayer. We have also talked about surrender as a gift, in chapter 3, about how our "yes" to the call to prayer is our first surrender to a power greater than ourselves, a surrender that is ultimately sweet and liberating.

In surrender we give up our self-centeredness in order to draw closer to the Divine. We put aside ego and desire in hopes of uniting our wills with the greater will of the Ineffable God. We come to understand, often quite slowly, that we simply aren't in control: We are not the directors of this pageantry called life; we are merely players. Or as Ruffing succinctly puts it, "God is God and we are not."

This may seem self-evident and simplistic to those of us who have been tending our spiritual pastures for some time. Of course God is God and we are not!

Really? Can we really be completely free of self-seeking and self-interest, pride and manipulation, attempts to control our and others' lives? Are we truly capable of discarding our willfulness and centering our entire being and life, including our needs and wants, around the benevolence of the Divine and not the machinations of our own conniving selves?

In fact, this is very difficult, indeed lifelong work, which will be a constant challenge to the integrity and meaningfulness of our prayer lives and our relationship with God. We will find ourselves surrendering again and again—surrendering our willfulness, our self-interest, our self-seeking—throughout our prayer in an effort to know and understand the Divine more fully and better align our will with God's will.

Because God is the living God, He can hear;
because He is a loving God, He will hear;
because He is our covenant God, He has bound
Himself to hear.

CHARLES HADDON SPURGEON

Fidelity

Finally, we come to the most essential and powerful ingredient of good prayer—fidelity or faithfulness. When we make the commitment to pray, we also make a commitment to enter into a relationship with the Divine. If prayer is going to work for us, if we are going to receive the extraordinary gift of experiencing the tangible and palpable God within and without us, we must keep "showing up" for prayer, and we must honor our relationship with the Divine.

With prayer and God, half measures will avail us nothing. Being faithful means we must throw ourselves wholeheartedly—body and soul, mind and emotions—into the act of prayer and into the arms of the Divine, over and over again. Even when we are hurting and angry. Even when our prayers are not answered. Even when the modern horrors of the late twentieth century rock our beliefs and sensibilities to their very core. Even when the long dark nights of our soul—and there will be those nights—seem interminable, relentless, unfathomable; too long and too dark. Even when the voice of God is silent. Especially when the voice of God is silent.

In the faithfulness, in the fidelity born and nurtured in our first "yes" to God and prayer, we must return to the altar of the Divine again and again, with absolute confidence that we will see the Light again.

FINAL THOUGHTS

The essence of prayer, even of a mystical experience, is the way we are altered to see everything from its life-filled dimension.

MATTHEW FOX

Prayer is the most extraordinary spiritual journey you will ever take. The rewards are limitless, the most potent of which is understanding with absolute conviction that we live and breathe in the presence of the Divine, always and everywhere. And that Presence is nothing less than unending love and compassion, joy and serenity. And more incredibly, that Presence lives not in the cosmos, but in our hearts.

We know this because we take our own prayer journey every day. And God has been good to us, so very good.

We have been comforted in the face of the violent and senseless deaths of those we love; we have known great physical and spiritual healing; we have been moved in our lives to find and do work that more clearly expresses the Divine's will for us; and we have been given the courage to keep doing that work, even when it gets hard and dry.

Prayer also has been the vehicle for us to be bathed unconditionally in the Divine's love and compassion, time and time again, when we are tired, hurting, fed up or lost. More wonderfully, we have been able to carry that love and compassion (not all the time, and never perfectly, but in our human fashion) to our families and friends, neighbors and strangers, in liturgy and in private conversations, in our writings and in our prayers. We have seen the face of God in those people with whom we break bread, lend a hand or an ear to, sit across from on a subway or bus, or bear witness to as they curl in a doorway in the midst of winter trying to find warmth and comfort. We have been loved and forgiven, and we love and forgive in return.

May God be good to you.

PART TWO

Prayers

6

Prayers to Open Oneself to the Ultimate Reality

Let me be quiet now, and kneel,
Who never knelt before,
Here, where the leaves paint patterns light
On a leaf-strewn forest floor;
For I, who saw no God at all
In sea or earth or air,
Baptized by Beauty, now look up
To see God everywhere.

ELLEN FRANCIS GILBERT

I bow, in the early morning, to the Full, the Eternal, that sun-hued
Purushottama beyond the darkness, in whose all-comprehending
form, this entire universe has been made to
flash forth, like a snake where there is only a rope.

HINDU PRAYER FROM *THE PRATASSMARANA STOTRA*

I offer Thee—
Every flower that ever grew,
Every bird that ever flew,
Every wind that ever blew,
Good God!
Every thunder rolling,
Every church bell tolling,
Every lead and sod.
Laudamus Te!

I offer Thee—
Every wave that ever moved,
Every heart that ever loved,
Thee, Thy Father's Well-Beloved,
Dear Lord!
Every river dashing,
Every lightning flashing,
Like an angel's sword.
Benedicimus Te!

I offer Thee—
Every cloud that ever swept
O'er the skies, and broke and wept
In rain, and with the flow'rets slept,
My King!
Each communicant praying,
Every angel staying
Before Thy throne to sing!
Adoramus Te!

I offer Thee—
Every flake of virgin snow,
Every spring the earth below,
Every human joy and woe.
My love!
O Lord! And all Thy glorious
Self, o'er death victorious,
Throned in heaven above.
Glorificamus Te!

MARY BROCAS HARRIS

*I laud that Being from whom the universe rises, in whom it flourishes
and into whom it again disappears; by whose light the universe
shines; whose splendour is ablaze with a Bliss that is all His own
and which Lord of all-beings, all-peace, permanent, free from all
action, the wise attain, never to be born again, driving away the
darkness of duality.*

HINDU PRAYER FROM *THE PRABODHACHANDRODAYA*

*How does the Moon wax?
How does the Moon wane?
Fifteen days does the Moon wax.
Fifteen days does the Moon wane.
So long is the waning, even as the waxing. . . .
Who is it, through whom the Moon
waxes and wanes, other than You?*

ZOROASTRIAN LITANY TO THE MOON

*O Lord, give me eyes which see nothing but Thy glory.
Give me a mind that finds delight in Thy service.
Give me a soul drunk in the wine of Thy wisdom.
O Lord, to find Thee is my desire,
But to comprehend Thee is beyond my strength.
Remembering Thee is solace to my sorrowing heart;*

Thoughts of Thee are my constant companions.
I call upon Thee night and day.
The flame of Thy love glows in the darkness of my night. . . .

ANSARI OF HERAT

In the name of Allah, the Beneficent, the Merciful.
Praise be to Allah, Lord of the Worlds,
The Beneficent, the Merciful.
Owner of the Day of Judgment,
Thee alone we worship; Thee alone we ask for help.
Show us the straight path,
The path of those whom Thou has favored;
Not the path of those who earn Thine anger nor
of those who go astray.

ISLAMIC HYMN OF PRAISE

Grant me the ability to be alone;
May it be my custom to go outdoors each day
Among the trees and grasses,

Among all growing things,
And there may I be alone,
To talk with the one
That I belong to.

RABBI NACHMAN OF BRATZLAV

O my God, my soul is a ship
Adrift in the seas of her own will,
Where there is no shelter from You except in You.

Appoint for her, O God, in the name of God,
Her course
And its harbor.

MUSLIM PRAYER

God is not to be comprehended by human thought,
Though we may try it a hundred thousand times.
Outward silence cannot still the mind's search for truth,
Though we absorb ourselves in meditation long and deep.
Our hunger for God can never be satisfied,

Even if we acquire everything the universe has to offer.
If we increase our wisdom beyond measure,
It is still not enough.
How, then, can we come to know the truth?
How can the veil of falsehood be torn asunder?
By following God's will, O Nanak,
Which is written within our hearts.

OPENING WORDS OF SIKH DEVOTIONS

Let nothing disturb you,
Let nothing dismay you.
All things pass.
God never changes.
Patience attains
all that it strives for.
She who has God
finds she lacks nothing.
God alone suffices.

ST. TERESA OF AVILA

I was utterly alone with the sun and the earth. Lying down on the
grass, I spoke in my soul to the earth, the sun, the air, and the distant
sea far beyond sight. I thought of the earth's firmness—I felt it bear
me up; through the grassy couch there came an influence as if I could
feel the great earth speaking to me. I thought of the wandering air—
its pureness, which is its beauty; the air touched me and gave me
something of itself. I spoke to the sea: though so far, in my mind I
saw it, green at the rim of the earth and blue in deeper ocean. . . .
I turned to the blue heaven over, gazing into its depth, inhaling its
exquisite colour and sweetness. The rich blue of the unattainable
flower of the sky drew my soul towards it, and there it rested, for pure
colour is rest of heart. By all these I prayed. . . . Then, returning, I
prayed by the sweet thyme, whose little flowers I touched with my
hand; by the slender grass; by the crumble of dry chalky earth
I took up and let fall through my fingers. Touching the crumble
of earth, the blade of grass, the thyme flower, breathing the

*earth-encircling air, thinking of the sea and the sky, holding out my
hand for the sunbeams to touch it, prone on the sward in token of
deep reverence, thus I prayed. . . .*

Richard Jefferies

*I place before my inward eyes myself with all that I am—my body,
soul, and all my powers—and I gather round me all the creatures
which God ever created in heaven, on earth, and in all the elements,
each one severally with its name, whether birds of the air, beasts of
the forest, fishes of the water, leaves and grass of the earth, or the
innumerable sands of the sea, and to these I add all the little specks of
dust which glance in the sunbeams, with all the little drops of water
which ever fell or are falling from dew, snow, or rain, and I wish that
each of these had a sweetly sounding stringed instrument, fashioned
from my heart's inmost blood, striking on which they might each send
up to our dear and gentle God a new and lofty strain of praise for
ever and ever. And then the loving arms of my soul stretch out and
extend themselves towards the innumerable multitude of all creatures,
and my intention is, just as a free and blithesome leader of a choir
stirs up the singers of his company, even so in turn all to good
account by inciting them to sing joyously, and to offer up their
hearts to God.*

Henrik Suso

7

Prayers of Invocation to Seek the Divine Presence

O God, you are my God,
early will I seek You.
My flesh longs for You,
my soul thirsts for You,
in a barren and dry land where there is no water.

PSALM 63:1

Holy Spirit
dwell in me,
that I may become prayer.

Whether I sleep or wake,
eat or drink,
labour or rest,
may the fragrance of prayer
rise, without effort, in my heart.
Purify my soul and never leave me,
so that the movements of my heart and mind
may, with voices full of sweetness,
sing in secret to God.

AFTER ST. ISAAC THE SYRIAN

Obeisance to the Sun, the support and the immanent soul
of everything, the very basis of the universe, the well-wisher
of the universe, the self-born, the eye of the whole world,
the foremost of the gods, of immeasurable splendour.

HINDU PRAYER FROM *THE SAMBAPURANA*

That I want Thee, only Thee—let my heart repeat without end.
All desires that distract me, day and night, are false and empty
to the core. As the night keeps hidden in its gloom the petition
for light, even thus in the depth of my unconsciousness rings
the cry—I want Thee, only Thee. As the storm still seeks its end
in peace when it strikes against peace with all its might,
even thus my rebellion strikes against Thy love and still
its cry is—I want Thee, only Thee.

RABINDRANATH TAGORE

Wherever I go—only Thou!
Wherever I stand—only Thou!
Just Thou;
again Thou;
always Thou!

HASIDIC SONG

May the words of my mouth
And the meditation of my heart
Be acceptable in your sight
O Lord, my strength and my redeemer.

PSALM 19:14

⚭

O God, give me faith, devotion and love,
So that I may constantly chant Thy Holy name.
Let my heart overflow with Thy love.
Let me realize what ravishment is there in Thy name,
And let my being be firmly rooted in Thee.
Thou are the indwelling Spirit: awaken my soul;
Let my soul be in holy communion with Thee,
And let that communion be constant.
Then, O merciful God, Thy supreme light will ever
shine in my life.

DADU

⚭

Alone with none but Thee, my God,
I journey on my way;
What need I fear when Thou art near,
O King of night and day?
More safe am I within Thy hand
Than if a host did round me stand.

ATTRIBUTED TO ST. COLUMBA

⚭

O Lord, I know not what to ask of Thee. Thou alone knowest
my true needs. Thou lovest me more than I myself know how to love.
I dare not ask either a cross or consolation: I can only wait on Thee.
My heart is open to Thee. Visit and help me, for Thy great mercy's

sake. Strike me and heal me, cast me down and raise me up.
I worship in silence Thy holy will and Thine inscrutable ways,
and offer myself as a sacrifice to Thee. I put all my trust in Thee.
I have no other desire than to fulfill Thy will. Teach me how to
pray. Pray Thou Thyself in me.

METROPOLITAN PHILARET OF MOSCOW

From the Unreal lead me to the real;
From darkness lead me to light;
From death lead me to deathlessness.

HINDU PRAYER

Adoration to the Supreme!
Veneration in the sacrifice!
Abundance and Purity.
The music is ready.

The Lord on High comes to enjoy Himself.
He will give us happiness,
benediction for our offerings,
and will cause everything to be for our good.

ANCIENT CHINESE HYMN TO THE SKY

8

Prayers of Gratitude and Thanksgiving

Father, we thank Thee for the night,
And for the pleasant morning light;
For rest and food and loving care,
And all that makes the day so fair.

Help us to do the things we should,
To be to others kind and good;
In all we do at work or play
To grow more loving every day.

REBECCA J. WESTON

I thank Thee, uncreated Sun,
That Thy bright beams on me have shined;
I thank Thee, who hast overthrown
My foes, and healed my wounded mind;
I thank Thee whose enlivening voice
Bids my freed heart in thee rejoice.

JOHANN SCHEFFLER (TRANSLATED BY JOHN WESLEY)

Not here for high and holy things
We render thanks to Thee,
But for the common things of earth,
The purple pageantry
Of dawning, and of dying days,
The splendour of the sea,

The royal robes of autumn moors,
The golden gates of spring,
The velvet of soft summer nights,
The silver glistening
Of all the million, million stars,
The silent song they sing.

G. A. STUDDERT-KENNEDY

I listen with reverence to the birdsong cascading
At dawn from the oasis, for it seems to me
There is no better evidence for the existence of God
Than in the bird that sings, though it knows not why,
From a spring of untrammeled joy that wells up in its heart.
Therefore I pray that no sky-hurled hawk may come
Plummeting down,
To silence the singer, and disrupt the Song.
That rhapsodic, assured, transcending Song
Which foretells and proclaims, when the Plan is worked out,
Life's destiny: the joyous, benign Intention of God.

AN ARAB CHIEFTAIN

I sing the earth, the firmly founded earth,
The honor'd nurse that tends us from our birth.
The dwellers of the air, the sea, the field,
Live on the treasures that she joys to yield.
Oh Earth! Thy generous deeds are greatly done,
Thine are good fruits and many a gallant son,
'Tis thine the springs of life to stop or move;

But happy, happy he who claims they love. . . .
Parent of Gods, the starry heaven's rich wife,
Oh grant me for my song a happy life;
And Oh, whene'er I touch the vocal string,
I'll think of Thee, and of another sing.

ANCIENT GREEK HYMN TO THE EARTH

Though our mouths were full of song as the seas, and our tongues
of exultation as the multitude of its waves, and our lips of praise as
the wide-extended firmament; though our eyes shone with light like
the sun and the moon, and our hands were spread forth like the eagle
of heaven, and our feet were swift as hinds, we should still be unable
to thank Thee and to bless Thy name, O Lord our God and God of
our fathers, for one thousandth or one ten-thousandth part of the
bounties which Thou hast bestowed upon our fathers and upon us.

THE HEBREW MORNING SERVICE

The sweetness of Thee is in the northern sky.
The beauty of Thee carries away hearts;
The love of Thee makes arms languid;
Thy beautiful form relaxes the hands;
And hearts are forgetful at the sight of Thee.
Thou art the sole one, who made all that is,
The solitary sole one, who made what exists,
From whose eyes mankind came forth,
And upon whose mouth the Gods came into being.

He who made herbage for the cattle,
And the fruit tree for mankind,
Who made that on which the fish in the river may live,
And the birds soaring in the sky.
He who gives breath to that which is in the egg,
Gives life to the son of the slug,
And makes that on which gnats may live,
And worms and flies in like manner;
Who supplies the needs of the mice in their holes,
And gives life to flying things in every tree.
Hail to Thee, who did all this!

ANCIENT EGYPTIAN HYMN TO THE SUN

Glory be to God for dappled things—
For skies of couple-colour as a brinded cow;
For rose-moles all in stipple upon trout that swim;
Fresh-firecoal chestnut-falls; finches' wings;
Landscape plotted and pieced—fold, fallow, and plough;
And all trades, their gear and tackle and trim.
All things counter, original, spare, strange;
Whatever is fickle, freckled (who knows how?)
With swift, slow; sweet, sour; adazzle, dim;
He fathers-forth whose beauty is past change:
Praise Him.

GERARD MANLEY HOPKINS

Abundant is the year, with much millet and much rice;
And we have our high granaries,
With myriads, and hundreds of thousands, and millions of
measures in them;
For spirits and sweet spirits,
To present to our ancestors, male and female,
And to supply all our ceremonies.
The blessings sent down on us are of every kind.

ANCIENT CHINESE PRAYER OF THANKSGIVING

Mother of the world, Earth! Obeisance again and again to you,
the wide, the bearer of large mountains. Obeisance to you,
O supporter and nurse of the world! Obeisance be to you,
the basis of the universe, the bearer of riches!

HINDU PRAYER FROM *THE VARAHAPURANA*

9

Prayers of Praise, Adoration and Faithfulness

O God, you are the unsearchable abyss of peace,
the ineffable sea of love,
and the fountain of blessings.
Water us with plenteous streams
from the riches of Your grace;
and from the most sweet springs of Your kindness,
make us children of quietness and heirs of peace.

FROM THE SYRIAN LITURGY OF ST. CLEMENT OF ALEXANDRIA

You are to be praised, O God of Zion,
and to You shall we make our commitment.
By Your strength You established the mountains,
and You are the hope of the ends of the earth.
You visit the earth and water it;
You make it richly fertile, providing grain for the people.
You crown the year with Your bounty,
the pastures overflow and the hills are clothed with joy!

The valleys stand so thick with corn,
they shout for joy and sing.

PSALM 65:1, 6, 9–13

O Lord of our senses, the world rejoices and becomes devoted
to You, the demons fly in all directions in fright,
and all perfected beings bow to You.

*And wherefore would they not bow, O Great Being, to You
who are greater than the creator and are the prime Creator?
Lord of all Gods who has no end, who dwells in the world and in
whom the world dwells! You are the Imperishable, the existent and the
nonexistent and that which is beyond both.*

*You are the first God; the Supreme Being, the oldest; You are the final
basis of this universe; You are the knower and the known; the supreme
state of salvation; O God of endless forms, by You and with You has
this universe been spread out.*
*You are Wind, Death, Fire, Water, Moon, Creator and the Father of
that creator also. Obeisance be to You a thousand times; repeated
and profuse be my obeisance to You.*

HINDU PRAYER FROM *THE BHAGAVADGITA*

*How can I tell of such love to me? You made me in Your image and
hold me in the palm of Your hand, Your cords of love, strong and
fragile as silk bind me and hold me.*
*Rich cords, to family and friends,
music and laughter echoing in memories,
light dancing on the water, hills rejoicing.
Cords that found me hiding behind carefully
built walls and led me out,
love that heard my heart break and despair and rescued me,
love that overcame my fears and doubts and released me.
The questions and burdens I carry You take,
to leave my hands free—to hold Yours, and others,
free to follow Your cords as they move and swirl in the breeze,
free to be caught up in the dance of Your love,*

finding myself in surrendering to You.
How can I tell of such love? How can I give to such love?
I am, here am I.

CATHERINE HOOPER

Praise the Lord.
Praise God in His sanctuary;
praise Him in His mighty heavens.

Praise Him for His acts of power;
praise Him for His surpassing greatness.
Praise Him with the sounding of the trumpet,
praise Him with the harp and lyre,
praise Him with tambourine and dancing,
praise Him with the strings and flute,
praise Him with the clash of cymbals,
praise Him with resounding cymbals.

Let everything that has breath praise the Lord.

PSALM 150:1–6

How excellent is Thy loving kindness, O God.
We commend to Thee, Lord, our impulses and our incentives,
Our intentions and our ventures,
Our going out and our coming in,
Our sitting down and our rising up.

How truly, meet, and right, and comely, and due,
In all and for all,
In all places, times and manners,
In every season, every spot,
Everywhere, always, altogether,
To remember Thee, to worship Thee,
To confess to Thee, to praise Thee,
To bless Thee, to give thanks to Thee,
Maker, Nourisher, Guardian, Governor,
Healer, Benefactor, Protector of all.

LANCELOT ANDREWES

You are holy, Lord, the only God,
and Your deeds are wonderful.
You are love, You are wisdom.
You are humility, You are endurance.
You are rest, You are peace.
You are joy and gladness.
You are all our riches, and You suffice for us.
You are beauty, You are gentleness.
You are our protector,
You are our guardian and defender.
You are courage,
You are our haven and hope.
You are our faith, our great consolation.
You are our eternal life, great and wonderful Lord,
God almightly, merciful Saviour.

ST. FRANCIS OF ASSISI (ABRIDGED)

All waters, the fountains as well as those flowing down in streams,
praise we.
All trees, the growing, adorned with tops, praise we.
The whole earth, praise we.
The whole heaven, praise we.
All Stars, the Moon and Sun, praise we.
All lights, without beginning, praise we.
All cattle, that which lives under the water, under the heaven,
the birds, the wide-stepping, the beasts with claws, praise we.
All the good pure creatures, working well for
Ahura-Mazda, praise we. . . .

Iranian Hymn to the Waters

Surely in the heavens and the earth there are signs for the faithful:
in Your own creation, and in the beasts that are scattered far and
near; signs for true believers, in the alternations of night and day, in
the sustenance Allah sends down from heaven with which He revives
the earth after its death, and in the marshalling of the winds,
signs for men of understanding.

The Koran

I see something of God each hour of the twenty-four, and each
moment then,
In the faces of men and women I see God, and in my own face
in the glass,
I find letters from God dropt in the street and every one is signed by
God's name,

And I leave them where they are, for I know that whereso'ere I go,
Others will punctually come for ever and ever.

WALT WHITMAN

Blessing and laughter and loving be yours.
The love of a Great God
who names you
and holds you
while the earth turns and the flowers grow,
this day
this night
this moment
and forever.

RUTH BURGESS

Lord Jesus, I am not an eagle. All I have are the eyes and the heart of
one. In spite of my littleness, I dare to gaze at the sun of love, and I
long to fly towards it.

ST. THERESE OF LISIEUX

Ah Lord, You can show Yourself to us as so beautiful and
tender, that our hearts cannot help but fall in love with You.
We yearn to be close to You. As we read the pages of Scripture,
it is as if You are whispering sweet words of affection in our ears. So
overwhelming is Your love that it leaves no space for mortal love
between men and women. O my dear Lord, my soul sighs for You.
And when I cannot hear You speak my heart is heavy with sadness.

Unless You are close beside me, I cannot rest or sleep.
Let me lie beside You, my head on Your bosom.

HENRIK SUSO

Who Thou art I know not,
But this much I know,
Thou hast set the Pleiades
In a silver row:
Thou hast sent the trackless winds
Loose upon their way;
Thou has reared a colored wall
Twixt the night and day;
Thou has made the flowers to bloom
And the stars to shine;
Hid rare gems of richest ore
In the tunneled mine:
But the chief of all Thy wondrous works,
Supreme of all Thy plan,
Thou has put an upward reach
In the heart of man.

HARRY KEMP

The shepherds sing; and shall I silent be?
My God, no hymns for Thee?
My soul's a shepherd too; a flock it feeds
Of thoughts, and words, and deeds;
The pasture is Thy word; the streams, Thy grace
Enriching all the place.

Shepherd and flock shall sing, and all my powers
Out-sing the day-light hours. . . .

GEORGE HERBERT

You are to me, O Lord,
What wings are to the flying bird.

A DISCIPLE OF RAMAKRISHNA

Beloved Pan, and all ye other gods who haunt this place, give me
beauty in the inward soul; and may the outward and inward (man)
be at one. May I reckon the wise to be the wealthy, and may I have
such a quantity of gold as a temperate man and he only can
carry—Anything more? This prayer, I think, is enough for me.

SOCRATES

O this beauty of the Universe!
How did You, my Lord, come to create it?
In what outburst of ecstasy
Allowed You Your Being to be manifested?
Some say You took fancy in the play of form,
Giving in delight Your Absolute Being an appearance.
Dadu understands You need him
In Thy play of creation.

DADU

What else can I do, a lame old man, but sing hymns to God?
If I were a nightingale, I would do the nightingale's part;
if I were a swan, I would do as a swan.
But now I am a rational creature, and I ought to praise
God: this is my work; I do it,
nor will I desert my post, so long as I am allowed to keep it. And I
exhort you to join me in this same song.

EPICTETUS, GREEK STOIC

God is in the water, God is in the dry land, God is in the heart.
God is in the forest, God is in the mountain, God is in the cave.

God is in the earth, God is in heaven. . . .
Thou art in the tree, Thou art in its leaves,
Thou art in the earth, Thou art in the firmament.

GOVIND SINGH, A SIKH PRAYER

O Thou shining one,
Thou knowst all our ways.
We utter praise of thee!
Thou art woman, Thou art man;
Thou art youth, thou art maiden. . . .
Thou art the dark blue bee,
Thou art the green parrot with red eyes,
Thou art the thunder-cloud,

The seasons, the seas.
Thou art our Father. Thou art our Mother.
Thou art our Beloved Friend.

Late have I loved You, O beauty so ancient and so new.
Too late have I loved You!
You were within me while I had gone outside to seek You.

Unlovely myself, I fell heedlessly upon all those lovely things
You had made.
And always You were with me, and I was not with You.
And all these beauties that held me far from You
would have existed not at all
Unless they had their being in You!

You called, You cried, You broke open my deafness.
You blazed, You gleamed, You drove away my blindness.
You sent Your fragrance, and I drew in my breath,
And I pant for You.

I tasted, and now I hunger and thirst.
You touched me, and now I burn with longing for Your peace.

ST. AUGUSTINE

It is glory enough for me
That I should be Your servant.
It is grace enough for me
That You should be my Lord.

ARABIC PRAYER

I slept and dreamt that life was joy
I woke and saw that life was service
I acted and behold! service was joy.

RABINDRANATH TAGORE

Lord, make me an instrument of Thy peace.
Where there is hatred, let me sow love.
Where there is injury, pardon.
Where there is doubt, faith.
Where there is sadness, joy.
O Divine Master, grant that I may not so much seek
to be consoled as to console;
to be understood, as to understand;
to be loved, as to love;
for it is in giving that we receive,
it is in pardoning that we are pardoned,
and it is in dying that we are born to Eternal Life.

ST. FRANCIS OF ASSISI

Abide with Me

Abide with me: fast falls the eventide;
The darkness deepens; Lord, with me abide:
When other helpers fail, and comforts flee,
Help of the helpless, oh, abide with me.

Swift to its close ebbs out life's little day;
Earth's joys grow dim, its glories pass away,
Change and decay in all around I see;
O Thou Who changest not, abide with me.
I need Thy presence every passing hour;
What but Thy grace can foil the tempter's power?
Who, like Thyself, my guide and stay can be?
Through cloud and sunshine, Lord, abide with me.

I fear no foe, with Thee at hand to bless:
Ills have no weight, and tears no bitterness.
Where is death's sting? Where, grave, thy victory?
I triumph still, if Thou abide with me.

Hold Thou Thy cross before my closing eyes:
Shine through the gloom and point me to the skies:
Heaven's morning breaks, and earth's vain shadows flee:
In life, in death, O Lord, abide with me.

HENRY FRANCIS LYTE (LYRICS TO POPULAR HYMN, WHOSE MUSIC
WAS COMPOSED BY WILLIAM HENRY MONK)

Lord, we know not what we ought to ask of Thee; Thou only know-
est what we need; Thou lovest us better than we know how to love
ourselves. O Father! Give to us, Thy children, that which we our-
selves know not how to ask. We would have no other desire than to
accomplish Thy will. Teach us to pray. Pray Thyself in us. . . .

FRANÇOIS DE LA FÉNELON

Lord, may I love all Thy creation, the whole and every grain of sand
in it. May I love every leaf, every ray of Thy light. May I love the
animals: Thou has given them the rudiments of thought and joy
untroubled. Let me not trouble it, let me not harass them, let me not
deprive them of their happiness, let me not work against Thine intent.
For I acknowledge unto Thee that all is like an ocean, all is flowing
and blending, and that to withhold any measure of love from any-
thing in Thy universe is to withhold that same measure from Thee.

ADAPTED FROM DOSTOEVSKY IN THE BROTHERS KARAMAZOV

Today I will walk out, today everything evil will
leave me, I will be as I was before. I will have a cool
breeze over me, I will travel with a light body. I will be happy
forever, nothing will hinder me. I walk with beauty before me,
I walk with beauty behind me, I walk with beauty above me,
I walk with beauty all around me, my words will be beautiful.

NAVAJO PRAYER

My heart is steadfast, O God,
my heart is steadfast;
I will sing and make music.
Awake, my soul!
Awake, harp and lyre!
I will awaken the dawn.
I will praise you, O Lord, among the nations;
I will sing of You among the peoples.

For great is Your love, reaching to the heavens;
Your faithfulness reaches to the skies.

Be exalted, O God, above the heavens;
let Your glory be over all the earth.

PSALM 57:7–11

10

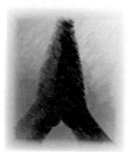

Prayers of
Benediction

I have thought upon Thee, O Lord,
when I was waking,
for Thou has been my helper.
Blessed art Thou, O Lord,
who madest the two Lights, Sun and Moon,
greater and lesser,
and the stars
for light, for signs, for seasons,
spring, summer, autumn, winter,
days, weeks, months, years,
to rule over day and night.

From The Greek Devotions of Bishop Andrewes

O Father of light and giver of all wisdom, bless every society formed
for the advancement and spread of Thy truth. . . . Let Thy word
have free course everywhere. May it never return unto Thee void, but
prosper abundantly, and accomplish all that for which Thou dost
send it. Give Thy servants health and strength, vigor of mind and
devotedness of heart. . . . Grant that thousands and tens of thousands
may rise up to call Thee blessed . . . and glorify Thy name. . . .

Hannah More

The God of Abraham praise,
Who reigns enthroned above;

Ancient of everlasting days,
And God of love;
Jehovah, Great I AM,
By earth and heaven confessed;
I bow and bless the sacred name;
Forever blessed.

THOMAS OLIVERS

. . . God of all peace and of all consolation, we desire to draw near
unto Thee, with humble, contrite, and grateful spirits.
We earnestly desire to be clothed with humility, as frail and
dependent creatures . . . to cultivate contrition . . . to cherish feelings
of unbounded gratitude.
Firmly believing that Thou art, rejoicing in the glorious attributes
of Thy nature, and viewing Thee as the author of every good and
of every perfect gift, we would call upon our souls
and all that is within us,
to magnify and bless Thy holy name.

H. MONTGOMERY

O Thou who art God over all, blessed for ever!
We venerate and adore Thee as the Almighty Creator and beneficent
Parent of innumerable worlds, infinitely good and infinitely wise and
just and true, the Fountain of life and light, and everlasting joy.
Thou, O God, art light, and in Thee is no darkness at all.

The earth is full of Thy riches, the world is resplendent
with Thy glory.
In everything around us we behold the emanations of Thy love.
In the garniture of the fields and in the stars of the firmament, we
trace the impressions of Thy sovereign beauty, consummate wisdom
and almighty power.
Where can we go from Thy presence, or whither shall we flee
from Thy spirit?
Vain are our thoughts that we can escape Thy vigilance,
or lie hid from Thine all-seeing eye.
Thy way is in the whirlwind and the storm, and the clouds
are the dust of Thy feet. . . .
There is no spot in the illimitable universe unvisited by Thy care,
and not a sparrow falleth to the ground without Thy knowledge.

W. H. DRUMMOND

Blessed art Thou, O Lord,
who didst create the firmament of heaven,
the heavens and the heaven of heavens,
the heavenly powers,
Angels, Archangels,
Cherubim, Seraphim,
waters above the heavens,
mists and exhalations,
for showers, dew, hail, snow as wool,
hoar frost as ashes, ice as morsels,
clouds from the ends of the earth,

lightnings, thunders, winds out of Thy treasures, storms;
waters beneath the heavens,
for drinking and for bathing.

FROM THE GREEK DEVOTIONS OF BISHOP ANDREWES

The Tree of Life

God be in my head
And in my understanding;
God be in my eyes
And in my looking;
God be in my mouth
And in my speaking;
God be in my heart
And in my thinking;
God be at my end
And at my departing.

PINTO AND WRIGHT, NO. 198, *THE SARUM PRIMER*

O Lord, You have searched me
and You know me.
You know when I sit and when I rise;
You perceive my thoughts from afar.
You discern my going out and my lying down;
You are familiar with all my ways.
Before a word is on my tongue
You know it completely, O Lord.
You hem me in—behind and before;
You have laid Your hand upon me.

Such knowledge is too wonderful for me,
too lofty for me to attain.
Where can I go from Your Spirit?
Where can I flee from Your presence?
If I go up to the heavens, You are there;
if I make my bed in the depths, You are there.
If I rise on the wings of the dawn,
if I settle on the far side of the sea,
even there Your hand will guide me,
Your right hand will hold me fast.

PSALM 139:1–10

Bless to me, O God, the earth beneath my feet,
Bless to me, O God, the path whereon I go,
Bless to me, O God, the people whom I meet,
Today, tonight and tomorrow.

A CELTIC BLESSING

May He who sets the holy and profane
Apart blot out our sins before His sight,
And make our numbers as the sand again,
And as the stars of night.

The day declineth like the palm tree's shade,
I call on God, who leadeth me aright.

The morning cometh—thus the watchman said—
       Although it now be night.

The righteousness is like Mount Tabor vast;
  O let my sins be wholly put to flight,
  Be they as yesterday, for ever past,
     And as a watch at night.

The man, son of Perez shall gladden our sight,
And we shall rejoice to the fullness of days.
Come in the joyousness, Crown of thy Lord;
Come, bringing peace to the folk of the Word;
Come where the faithful in gladsome accord,
Hail Thee as Sabbath-Bride, Queen of the days.
Come where the faithful are hymning Thy praise,
Come as a bride cometh, Queen of the days!

FROM THE HAVDALAH SERVICE AT THE END OF THE SABBATH

11

Prayers of Petition

Dear God, be good to me;
the sea is so large,
and my boat is so small.

TRADITIONAL PRAYER OF BRETON FISHERMEN

O Mother! Constantly contemplating within myself, crest to feet,
each limb of Yours which bestows welfare on the universe, and rocked
on the billows of an ocean of bliss, I count not the days passing.
Let me not be in a place devoid of Your presence; let me not learn any
lore which does not enlighten me on the truth of You; let not my
family and descendents be ever bereft of devotion to Your feet;
let me not have a life empty of Your contemplation.

HINDU PRAYER FROM *THE ANANDASAGARASTAVA*

May the clouds rain at the proper time; may Earth be rich
with crops; may this country be free from riots and
may the spiritual teachers be free from fear.
May everybody be happy; may everybody be free from disease;
may everybody come by happy events; may nobody
have any misery.
May everybody surmount difficulties; may everybody realise his
ambitions; may everybody be joyous everywhere.

HINDU BENEDICTION

My God, I can do no more!
Be for me the one who can!

MADAME ACARIE

Help me today to realise that You will be speaking to me through
the events of the day, through people, through things, and through
all creation.
Give me ears, eyes and heart to perceive You, however veiled your
presence may be.
Give me insight to see through the exterior of things to the
interior truth.
Give me Your Spirit of discernment!
O Lord, Thou knowest how busy I must be this day.
If I forget Thee, do not forget me!

JACOB ASTLEY

Be Thou a bright flame before me,
Be Thou a guiding star above me,
Be Thou a smooth path below me,
Be Thou a kindly shepherd behind me,
Today—tonight—and for ever.

ST. COLUMBA

Give me a good digestion, Lord,
And also something to digest.

Give me a healthy body, Lord,
With sense to keep it at its best.

Give me a healthy mind, Lord,
To keep the good and pure in sight,
Which, seeing sin, is not appalled,
But finds a way to set it right.

Give me a mind that is not bored,
That does not whimper, whine or sigh;
Don't let me worry overmuch
About the fussy thing called I.

Give me a sense of humor, Lord,
Give me the grace to see a joke,
To get some happiness from life
And pass it on to other folk.

AUTHOR UNKNOWN; FROM A TABLET IN CHESTER CATHEDRAL, ENGLAND

May the Goddess of Intellect come to us in love. She who
comprehends everything, is auspicious and is favourably disposed
to us; being blessed by You, we shall, with our heroic following, shun
lowly talk and speak at the end of the sacrifice about the Supreme.
O Goddess of Intellect, the person who is blessed by you, becomes a

[person] of vision, becomes Brahma Himself; through you, splendour
comes to [us]; [we] attain wonderful riches. Bless us,
O Goddess of Intellect, with such riches.

HINDU PRAYER FROM THE VEDAS

When the heart is hard and parched up, come upon me
with a shower of mercy.
When grace is lost from life, come with a burst of song.
When tumultuous work raises its din on all sides
shutting me out from beyond, come to me,
my Lord of silence, with Thy peace and rest.
When my beggarly heart sits crouched, shut up in a corner, break
open the door, my king, and come with the ceremony of a king.
When desire blinds the mind with delusion and dust, O Thou
holy One, Thou wakeful, come with Thy light and Thy thunder.

RABINDRANATH TAGORE

O Lord, keep us sensitive to the grace that is around us. May the
familiar not become neglected. May we see Thy goodness in our
daily bread, and may the comforts of our home take our thoughts
to the mercy-seat of God. . . .

J. H. JOWETT

God, that madest earth and heaven,
Darkness and light,
Who the day for toil has given,
For rest the night:
May Thine angel-guards defend us,
Slumber sweet Thy mercy send us,
Holy dreams and hopes attend us,
This livelong night.

Guard us waking, guard us sleeping,
And, when we die,
May we in Thy mighty keeping,
All peaceful lie:
When the last dread call shall wake us,
Do not Thou, our God, forsake us,
But to reign in glory take us
With Thee on high.

R. Heber and R. Whateley

God, grant me the
Serenity to accept the things I cannot change,
Courage to change the things I can, and
Wisdom to know the difference.

Reinhold Niebuhr

Supreme Lord,
let there be peace in the sky and in the air,
peace in the plant world and in the forests;
let the cosmic powers be peaceful;
let Brahma be peaceful;
let there be undiluted and all-fulfilling peace everywhere.

THE ATHARVA VEDA

O ye Knowledge-Holding Deities, pray hearken unto me;
Lead me on the Path, out of Your great love.
When I am wandering in the Sangsara,
because of intensified propensities,
On the bright light-path of the Simultaneously-born Wisdom,
May the bands of Heroes, the Knowledge-Holders, lead me;
May the bands of the Mothers, the Dakinis, be my rear guard;
May they save me from the fearful ambuscades of the Bardo,
And place me in the pure Paradise Realms.

TIBETAN PRAYER FOR THE TRANSMIGRATION

12

Prayers for Others

God of pity, God of peace and love, forgive,
oh forgive the slaveholders!
Great is their guilt, but infinite is Thy pity.
Open up in the desert of their souls the living fountain of charity.
May the angel of penitence descend . . .
and between them and his sentence
May the prayer arise of those who suffer,
as I suffer, for Thy holy cause,
Thy sacred truth, for the emancipation of nations
and the human soul!

GIUSEPPE MAZZINI

Thou who art Lord of all the tender pities,
Mercy Incarnate, human and Divine,
How could we write Thy Name upon these cities
Wherein Thy children live like herded swine?

Would not those eyes that saw their angels gazing
Into the brightness of the Father's face
Turn on this slum, with Love and Fury blazing,
Shriveling our souls with shame of such a place?

Where are My children, those the Father gave you?
What have you done with babes that bore My Name?
Was it for this I suffered so to save you,
Must I for ever burn for you in shame?

G. A. STUDDERT-KENNEDY

How excellent is Thy mercy, O Lord;
If I have hope, it is in Thy mercy,
O let me not be disappointed of my hope.
Moreover we beseech Thee,
Remember all, Lord, for good;
Have pity upon all, O Sovereign Lord,
Be reconciled with us all.
Give peace to the multitudes of Thy people;
Scatter offences;
Abolish wars;
Stop the uprisings of heresies.
Thy peace and love vouchsafe to us, O God our Saviour,
The Hope of all the ends of the earth. . . .

FROM THE GREEK DEVOTIONS OF BISHOP ANDREWES

Not thus can man be saved, by bread alone;
The hunger in his heart is Infinite,
And craves Infinity for food; the beast
Within him thrives on bread and starves the soul,
And this soul-hunger goads the beast, and drives
The whole man downwards into Hell, where lusts
And new desires wake to life, as vermin
Breed in putrid flesh, and crawling there become
Fat breeders of a pestilential brood
More filthy than themselves. So fares man's soul
That starves within a body fully fed.
Men grow luxurious, and cruelty,

More cruel in disguise of Beauty's robes,
Grows callously refined, and blinds their eyes to Love.
There lust is satiated not,
But craves the sting of grosser lusts, to prick
The jaded appetite to life. My God!
I see it all: I dare not give man bread,
Unless I give him more. He must have God—
Must learn to read God's message in the stars
Above him, and the stones beneath. His bread
Must be to him the Body of His God,
The sacrament of fuller life, which he
Takes on his knees, and with a thankful heart
Made kind by gratitude.

G. A. Studdert-Kennedy

Peace I leave with you; my peace I give unto you.
Not as the world giveth, give I unto you.
Let not your heart be troubled, neither let it be afraid.

Jesus Christ (John 14:27)

May no one who encounters me
ever have an insignificant contact.
May the mere fact of our meeting
contribute to the fulfillment of their wishes.

May I be a protector of the helpless,
a guide to those travelling the path,

a boat to those wishing to cross over,
or a bridge or a raft.

May I be a lamp for those in darkness,
a home for the homeless,
and a servant to the world.

FROM THE BODHICARYAVATARA OF SHANTIDEVA, BUDDHIST SCRIPTURE

. . . O Helper of the helpless, bring the wanderer home, and give
health to the sick, and deliverance to the captive. Sustain the aged,
comfort the weak-hearted, set free those whose souls are bound in
misery and iron; remember all those who are in affliction, necessity,
and emergency everywhere. Let us dwell with Thee in peace, as
children of light, and in Thy light, Lord, let us see the light.
Direct, O Lord, in peace, the close of our life, trustfully, fearlessly,
and, if it be Thy will, painlessly. Gather us when Thou wilt, into the
abode of Thy chosen, without shame, or stain, or sin. . . .

ROWLAND WILLIAMS

Watch Thou, dear Lord, with those who wake, or watch, or weep
tonight, and give Thine angels charge over those who sleep.
Tend Thy sick ones, O Lord; rest Thy weary ones; bless Thy dying
ones; soothe Thy suffering ones; shield Thy joyous ones; and all for
Thy Love's sake.

ST. AUGUSTINE

Great Sun Power, I am praying for my people
that they may be happy in the summer and that they may
live through the cold of winter. Many are sick and in want.
Pity them and let them survive. Grant that they may live long and
have abundance. . . . If we make mistakes, pity us.
Help us, Mother Earth, for we depend upon your goodness.
Let there be rain to water the prairies, that the grass
may grow long and the berries be abundant.
O Morning Star! When you look down upon us, give us peace and
refreshing sleep. Great Spirit!
Bless our children, friends, and visitors through a happy life.
May our trails lie straight and level before us.
Let us live to be old.
We are all your children and ask these things with good hearts.

NATIVE AMERICAN HYMN TO THE SUN

13

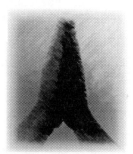

Prayers for Healing

O Holy Spirit, O Eternal God, O Christ, O Love, come Thou into
my heart; by Thy power draw it unto Thee, my God, and give me
charity with fear. Protect me Thou, O ineffable Love, from every evil
thought; inflame me and permeate me with Thy exquisite love, so that
every pain may become a ray of light! My Holy Father and my
sweet Lord, help me now in all of my ministries. Christ, Love, Amen.

CATHERINE OF SIENA

O the grace of God! O the purity of God! The goodness of God!
Is it possible, my Beloved, that man can love Thee, without
experiencing consolation and happiness in this love?
To me every event is God; and whether it be joyful or
afflictive, I receive it with equal gratitude, knowing that
He will send me only what I need.
To me every object is God. I do not go into distinctions,
and say, this is mine, or that is mine.
But I say, God is mine; everything belongs to God;
and I have an inward conviction, which is better understood than
expressed, that in the possession of God I have all that God has.
O my Beloved! is it possible that Thou hast thus called me to Thyself
with so great goodness? Is it possible that Thou hast delivered me
from my doubt and anguish; and in a moment of time hast imparted
a knowledge greater than language can express?
I have faith in Thee, O my God, that Thou wilt not leave me, that
Thou wilt not permit me to go astray; but will keep me in all inward
thought, as well as in all outward word and action.

CATHERINE OF GENOA

Speak to me low, my Savior, low and sweet
From out the hallelujas, sweet and low,
Lest I should fear and fall, and miss thee so
Who are not missed by any that entreat.
Speak to me as to Mary at thy feet—
And if no precious gums my hands bestow,
Let my tears drop like amber, while I go
In reach of thy divinest voice complete
In humanest affection—thus, in sooth,
To lose the sense of losing! As a child,
Whose song-bird seeks the wood for evermore,
Is sung to in its stead by mother's mouth;
Till, sinking on her breast, love-reconciled,
He sleeps the faster that he wept before.

ELIZABETH BARRETT BROWNING

Eternal God, the author and supporter of life,
we humble ourselves in Thy sight,
impressed with a sense of our frail and transitory nature.
O teach us, we implore Thee, so to number our days,
that we may apply our hearts unto wisdom.
Teach us to withdraw our affections from things on the earth,
and fix them on things above.

Teach us to prepare ourselves, and ever
hold ourselves prepared, for that great change
which may come as a thief in the night.
Lead our feeble and wavering hearts to fix themselves firmly on Thee,
that while we are of the earth earthy,
we may feel ourselves allied with heaven. . . .

J. R. BEARD

O most adorable and incomprehensible Being!
whose splendor no eye can bear, no thought conceive,
Whose power rideth on the whirlwind,
Whose wisdom discerneth the hidden things of darkness,
Whose goodness poureth on our hearts their gladness;
Whom to adore is solemn joy,
Whom to trust is unfailing safety,
Whom to love is peace eternal:
Before Thee we are nothing; without Thee we can do nothing.
In dependence on Thee is all our strength;
In the beamings of Thy glory is all our light;
In prostrating our wills before Thine is our noblest elevation.

O God of love, whose glory pervadeth all things!
Whose presence is the light of other worlds,
Whose mercy dwelleth among the abodes of men;
We trace Thy footsteps throughout creation,
Thy providence in all events. . . .
Amid the weaknesses and wants of our nature,
May we look on Thee who hath taken away our infirmities,
and be healed.

JAMES MARTINEAU

Almighty God! It is our rejoicing that we are the creatures of
Thy hand and the subjects of Thy care,
and we would seek above all things a nearer and purer communion
with Thee. . . .
Too often we have slighted Thy goodness; too often we have lost sight
of the great end for which we were created, and in pursuing the trifles
and follies of earth, wasted those precious moments which should
have brought us nearer to Thee, and nearer to heaven.
O may we be led to redeem the time, which may yet remain, in the
working out of our salvation.
May this world no longer delude us.
May temptations no longer have power to draw us aside from the
race of glory that is set before us.
But in all things may we feel and act as immortal beings.
While day by day is stealing from our little sum of life,
may we find our treasure of sweet thoughts,
from duties done, continually increasing.
While year after year is running by, and leaving us less and less
to be enjoyed on earth, may we find our hopes of heaven
continually growing in our souls. . . .
And when our troubles here are past, and we descend the dark valley,
may we be supported by Thine arm
and cheered by the light of Thy love.

W. GASKELL

I know no Mantra, Yantra, or Stotra; I know no invocation or contemplation; I know no stories in Your praise; I know not Your
Mudras, not even how to cry out to You; simply, I know, Mother, to
run after You, which itself destroys all my distress. . . .

*Goddess Durga, ocean of compassion, I think of You only when I am
immersed in calamities; do not take it as roguery on my part; only
when hungry and thirsty do children think of their Mother.*

HINDU PRAYER FROM THE DEVYAPARADHAKSHAMAPANA STOTRA

Lord,
*I am tearing the heart of my soul in two.
I need You to come
and lie there Yourself
in the wounds of my soul.*

MECHTILD OF MAGDBURG

*Grant me your special protection, let me partake of your privileges,
and by virtue of your greatness and your right of property over me,
let me obtain what I in my smallness am unworthy of obtaining. In
honor of that wondrous moment when God was made Incarnate and
you were made the Mother, I put myself wholly in your hands. . . .
O Virgin and Mother! O sacred temple of Divinity! O wonder of
earth and Heaven! O Mother of my Lord, I belong to you because of
your greatness and generosity, but wish to belong to you because of
my dedication, resolution, and choice. . . .*

CARDINAL DI BERULLE

Thou perfect master,
Who shinest upon all things and all men,
As gleaming moonlight plays upon a thousand waters
at the same time!
Thy great compassion does not pass by a single creature.
Steady and quietly sails the great ship of compassion across
the sea of sorrow.
Thou art the great physician for a sick and impure world,
In pity giving the invitation to the "Paradise of the West."

BUDDHIST VERSE FROM *MASSES FOR THE DEAD, AMIDISTA*

14

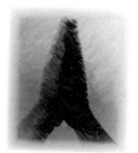

Prayers of Lamentation

Lord of the Winds, I cry to Thee,
I that am dust;
And blown about with every gust
I fly to Thee.

Lord of the Waters, unto Thee I call
I that am weed upon the waters borne
And by the waters torn,
Tossed by the waters at Thy feet I fall.

MARY COLERIDGE

Whence shall my tears begin?
What first-fruits shall I bear
Of earnest sorrow for my sin?
Or how my woes declare?
O Thou! the merciful and gracious One,
Forgive the foul transgressions I have done.

I lie before Thy door,
O turn me not away!
Nor in my old age give me o'er
To Satan for a prey!
But ere the end of life and term of grace,
Thou Merciful, my many sins efface!

ANDREW OF CRETE

Be pleased, O Lord, to deliver me,
Make haste, O Lord, to help me.
Magnify Thy mercies upon me,
O Thou who savest them that trust in Thee.
I said, Lord, have mercy upon me,
heal my soul, for I have sinned against Thee;
I have sinned, but I am confounded,
and I turn from my evil ways,
and I turn unto mine own heart,
and with my whole heart I turn unto Thee;
and I seek Thy face,
and I beseech Thee, saying,
I have sinned, I have commited iniquity,
I have done unjustly. . . .
O hear the prayer
and the supplication of Thy servant;
and be propitious towards Thy servant and heal his soul.

FROM THE GREEK DEVOTIONS OF BISHOP ANDREWES

We have questioned Thy goodness, O God,
We have murmured at Thy ways.
Pardon, tender Father, pardon Thy ignorant children.
With our limited faculties, we see but the present hour, and
comprehend not Thy merciful designs.
Come Thou into our hearts, and aid our weakness, enlighten our
understanding, strengthen our faith, raise from our sight, though but
for a moment, the veil that hides from us the secrets of eternity.

Teach us to see Thee in misfortune, as well as in prosperity;
in sorrow, as well as in joy. . . .
In mercy hear us, O our God and Father. . . .

                                       M. DUBY

Heavenly Father! with sorrow must we confess. . . .
Too often we have slighted Thy goodness;
Too often we have lost sight of the great end
for which we were created,
And in pursuing the trifles and follies of earth,
wasted those precious moments which
Should have brought us nearer to Thee, and nearer to heaven. . . .
May this world no longer delude us.
But in all things may we feel and act as immortal beings.
While day by day is stealing from our little sum of life,
May we find our treasure of sweet thoughts,
from duties done, continually increasing. . . .
May we find our hopes of heaven continually growing
in our souls,
So that when the evil days draw nigh,
We may still have a peace which the world cannot give,
And calmly wait all the days of our appointed time,
till our change comes.
And when our troubles here are past,
And we descend the dark valley,
May we be supported by Thine arm
and cheered by the light of Thy love. . . .

                                    W. GASKELL

As the deer pants for streams of water,
so my soul pants for You, O God.
My soul thirsts for God, for the living God.

When can I go and meet with God?
My tears have been my food day and night,
while men say to me all day long,
"Where is your God?"
These things I remember
as I pour out my soul:
how I used to go with the multitude,
leading the procession to the house of God,
with shouts of joy and thanksgiving
among the festive throng.

Why are you downcast, O my soul?
Why so disturbed within me?
Put your hope in God,
for I will yet praise Him,
my Savior and my God.

PSALM 42:1–6

O God, help me to think of Thee in this bitter trial. Thou knowest
how my heart is rent with grief. In my weakness, tested so severely in
soul by this visitation, I cry unto Thee, Father of all life: give me
fortitude to say with Thy servant Job: "The Lord hath given; the
Lord hath taken away; blessed be the name of the Lord."

Forgive the thoughts of my rebellious soul. Pardon me in these first hours of my grief, if I question Thy wisdom and exercise myself in things too high for me. Grant me strength to rise above this trial, to bear with humility life's sorrows and disappointments.
Be nigh unto me, O God. Bring consolation and peace to my soul. Praised art thou, O God, who comfortest the mourners.

UNION PRAYER BOOK

Listen to my prayer, O God,
do not ignore my plea;
hear me and answer me.
My thoughts trouble me and I am distraught
at the voice of the enemy,
at the stares of the wicked;
for they bring down suffering upon me
and revile me in their anger.

My heart is in anguish within me;
the terrors of death assail me.
Fear and trembling have beset me;
horror has overwhelmed me.

I said, "Oh, that I had the wings of a dove!
I would fly away and be at rest—
I would flee far away
and stay in the desert;
I would hurry to my place of shelter,
far from the tempest and storm."

But I call to God,
and the Lord saves me.
Evening, morning and noon
I cry out in distress,
and He hears my voice.

PSALM 55:1–8, 16–19

Lord, in this hour of tumult,
Lord, in this night of fears,
Keep open, oh, keep open
My eyes, my ears!

Not blindly, not in hatred,
Lord, let me do my part;
Keep open, oh, keep open,
My mind, my heart!

HERMANN HAGEDORN

My God, my God, why have You forsaken me?
Why are You so far from saving me,
so far from the words of my groaning?
O my God, I cry out by day, but You do not answer,
by night, and am not silent. . . .

Yet You brought me out of the womb;
You made me trust in You
even at my mother's breast.
From birth I was cast upon You;
from my mother's womb You have been my God.
Do not be far from me,
for trouble is near
and there is no one to help.

PSALM 22:1–3, 9–11

15

Prayers of Reconciliation

Our Father, from Thy throne on high
Behold in love Thy people here;
Regard the contrite, humble cry,
The joy, the gratitude, the tear.
This temple, holy may it be;
Our offerings ever here receive;
And when our prayers ascend to Thee,
Our sins, our sins, great God, forgive!

Have pity, Lord, on all oppressed
With pain, anxiety or grief;
O, ever comfort the distressed
And to Thy captive grant relief.
Beneath Thy kind protecting wing
May we forever, ever live;
Hear Thou the offerings now we bring,
And when Thou hearest, Lord, forgive!

MARY H. CUTTS, FROM *SOLOMON'S PRAYER*

Essence beyond essence, Nature increate,
Framer of the world,
I set Thee, Lord, before my face,
and I lift up my soul unto Thee.
I worship Thee on my knees,
and humble myself under Thy mighty hand.
I stretch forth my hands unto Thee,
my soul gaspeth unto Thee as a thirsty land.
I smite on my breast
and say with the Publican,

God be merciful to me a sinner,
the chief of sinner;
to the sinner above the Publican,
be merciful as to the Publican.
Father of mercies,
I beseech Thy fatherly affection,
despise me not. . . .

FROM THE GREEK DEVOTIONS OF BISHOP ANDREWES

Lord, You are like a wild flower. You spring up in places where we least expect You. The bright colour of Your grace dazzles us. When we reach down to pluck You, hoping to possess You for our own, You blow away in the wind. And if we tried to destroy You, by stamping on You and kicking You, You would come back to life. Lord, may we come to expect You anywhere and everywhere. May we rejoice in Your beauty. Far from trying to possess You, may You possess us. And may You forgive us for all the times when we have sinned against You.

HENRIK SUSO

Create in me a pure heart, O God,
and renew a steadfast spirit within me.
Do not cast me from Your presence
or take Your Holy Spirit from me.
Restore to me the joy of Your salvation
and grant me a willing spirit, to sustain me.

O Lord, open my lips,
and my mouth will declare Your praise.

You do not delight in sacrifice, or I would bring it;
You do not take pleasure in burnt offerings.
The sacrifices of God are a broken spirit;
a broken and contrite heart,
O God, You will not despise.

PSALM 51:10–12, 15–17

O God of earth and altar,
Bow down and hear our cry,
Our earthly rulers falter,
Our people drift and die;
The walls of gold entomb us,
The swords of scorn divide,
Take not Thy thunder from us
But take away our pride!

From all that terror teaches,
From lies of tongue and pen,
From all the easy speeches
That comfort cruel men,

From sale and profanation
Of honor and the sword,
From sleep and from damnation
Deliver us, Good Lord!

GILBERT KEITH CHESTERTON

To you, O Lord, I lift up my soul;
in You I trust, O my God.
Do not let me be put to shame,
nor let my enemies triumph over me. . . .

Show me Your ways, O Lord,
teach me Your paths;
guide me in Your truth and teach me,
for You are God my Savior,
and my hope is in You all day long.
Remember, O Lord, Your great mercy and love,
for they are from of old.
Remember not the sins of my youth
and my rebellious ways;
according to Your love remember me,
for You are good, O Lord.

PSALM 25:1–2, 4–7

I am a great sinner, O Cloud-of-Mercy!
Take care of me, one lowly in heart.
Again and again, moment after moment,
I place my head at Your feet.

I will use my body for a wave offering
Over Your feet.
I am Your servant.
Do not disappoint me.

SIXTEENTH–CENTURY HINDU PRAYER

With affected hearts,
we look at the space,
in sincere hope,
with respectful sentiments.
Coming out of the mysterious,
the Genii descend, invisible.
With veneration, the emperor
and his ministers raise their eyes.
We have done all that can be done
to open the way to the Genii,
to cause these transcendental intelligences to come,
to entertain them with respect,
after having evoked them in the azure heights,
and in the dark depths.

Ancient Chinese Buddhist Prayer to the Genii

O God, You are my God,
earnestly I seek You;
my soul thirsts for You,
my body longs for You,
in a dry and weary land
where there is no water.
I have seen You in the sanctuary
and beheld Your power and Your glory.
Because Your love is better than life,
my lips will glorify You.
I will praise You as long as I live,
and in Your name I will lift up my hands.

My soul will be satisfied as with the richest of foods;
with singing lips my mouth will praise You.

On my bed I remember You;
I think of You through the watches of the night.
Because You are my help,
I sing in the shadow of Your wings.
My soul clings to You;
Your right hand upholds me.

PSALM 63:1–8

O Viracocha! Lord of the universe;
Whether Thou art male,
Whether Thou art female,
Lord of reproduction,
Whatsoever Thou mayest be,
O Lord of divination,
Where art Thou?

Thou mayest be above,
Thou mayest be below,
Or perhaps around
Thy splendid throne and scepter.
Oh, hear me!
From the sky above,
In which Thou mayest be,
From the sea beneath,
In which Thou mayest be,
Creator of the world,
Maker of all men;
Lord of all Lords,

My eyes fail me
For longing to see Thee;
For the sole desire to know Thee.
Might I behold Thee,
Might I know Thee,
Might I consider Thee.
Might I understand Thee.
Oh, look down upon me,
For Thou knowest me.

The sun—the moon—
The day—the night—
Spring—winter,
Are not ordained in vain
By Thee, O Viracocha!
They all travel
To the assigned place;
They all arrive
At their destined ends,
Withersoever Thou pleasest.

Thy royal scepter
Thou holdest.
Oh, hear me,
Oh, choose me,
Let it not be
That I should tire,
That I should die.

INCA HYMN TO THE SUPREME GOD, VIRACOCHA

16

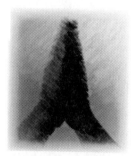

Prayers as Life Draws to a Close

∽

*O Lord, Thou has taken from us the fear of death; Thou makest the
close of life, the commencement of a new and truer life. For a while
Thou wilt suffer our bodies to sleep, and then will call us with the
trumpet at the end of time.*

*Now send Thee an angel of light besides me; bid him take my hand
and lead me to the place of rest, where there is water for my thirst
beside the dwelling place of the Holy Fathers.*

*If in the weakness of the flesh I have sinned in word, or deed, or
thought, forgive me Thou, O Lord, for Thou hast power to forgive
sins on earth. When I am divested of my body, may I stand before
Thee with my soul unspotted; receive it, Thou, without faults or sins,
in Thine own hands.*

MACRINA THE YOUNGER

∽

*O Lord, God Almighty! My life is nigh unto its end. Strengthen me
and hearken unto me and pity me
and those who stand grieving round about me,
and show unto me Thy mercy even as unto all those who have been
well pleasing unto Thee. And I pray Thee, Lord, do not Thou desert
me because my father and my mother have forsaken me, but
Thou, O Lord, my God, raise me up.*

*And do Thou guard me in the short time of this life, and guide me
into the haven of Thine intent, even as Thou didst lead the Children
of Israel into their flight from Egypt, through the sea and through
dry land. . . . O Lord! deign to hear me and quench the wrath of
this tyrant, who hath risen up against me and destroy his power
and will, for Thou, O Lord, knowest the nature of man,
that it is not able to endure captivity.*

JULIANA OF NICOMEDIA

Day is fled and gone,
life too is going,
this lifeless life.
Night cometh,
and cometh death,
the deathless death.
Near as is the end of day,
so too the end of life;
We then, also remembering it,
beseech of Thee
for the close of our life,
that Thou wouldst direct it in peace . . .
acceptable, sinless, shameless,
and, if it please Thee, painless,
Lord, O Lord,
gathering us together
under the feet of Thine Elect,
when Thou wilt, and as Thou wilt,
only without shame and sins. . . .
Blessed art Thou, O Lord, our God,
the God of our fathers,
who hast created the changes of days and nights,
who givest songs in the night,
who hast delivered us from the evil of this day,
who hast not cut off like a weaver my life,
nor from day even to night made an end of me.

FROM THE GREEK DEVOTIONS OF BISHOP ANDREWES

Take the last kiss—the last forever!
Yet render thanks amidst your gloom;
He, severed from his home and kindred,
Is passing onwards to the tomb.
For earthly labor, earthly pleasures
And carnal joys, he cares no more;
Whose are his kinsfolk and acquaintance?
They stand upon another shore.
Let us say, around him pressed,
Grant him, Lord, eternal rest!

JOHN OF DAMASCUS

Earthly cavern, to thy keeping
We commit our Brother's dust;
Keep it safely, softly sleeping,
Till our Lord demand thy trust.

Sweetly sleep, dear Saint. . . .
Thou, with us, shalt wake from Death;
Hold he cannot, though he seize us;
We his power defy by faith.

JOSEPH HART

Almighty God, the Author of our being . . .
May it please Thee to comfort and bless,
in an especial manner,
parents who have suffered the loss of good and beloved children,
and weep over their early and untimely graves.
Teach them to reflect, that they, for whom they mourn,
have made a blessed exchange; and having been delivered from the
cares and troubles of this vain life,
now rest with Thee.
And as each link is severed from that chain which binds us
to this world,
as each earthly stay glides from beneath our hands,
may we endeavor to prepare for our departure,
and wait, with patience and resignation,
"all the days of our appointed time, till our change come"—
hoping again to meet those we loved upon this earth,
and whose dear image is ever cherished within our hearts,
in that more blissful state, "where God shall wipe away all tears
from our eyes; and there shall be no more death,
neither sorrow nor crying."

J. C. LEDLIE

'Twere heaven enough to fill my heart
If only one would stay,
Just one of all the million joys
God gives to take away.

If I could keep one golden dawn,
The splendour of one star,
One silver glint of yon bird's wing
That flashes from afar;

If I could keep the least of things
That make me catch my breath
To gasp with wonder at God's world
And hold it back from death,

It were enough; but death forbids.
The sunset flames to fade,
The velvet petals of this rose
Fall withered—brown—decayed.

"O Grave, where is Thy victory?"
"O Death, where is Thy sting?"
Thy victory is ev'rywhere,
Thy sting's in ev'rything.

G. A. STUDDERT-KENNEDY

Day is dying in the west;
Heaven is touching earth with rest;
Wait and worship while the night
Sets the evening lamps alight,
Through all the sky.
Lord of life, beneath the dome
Of the universe, Thy home,
Gather us, who seek Thy face

To the fold of Thy embrace,
For Thou are nigh.
While the deepening shadows fall,
Heart of love, enfolding all,
Through the glory and the grace
Of the stars that veil Thy face,
Our hearts ascend.
When forever from our sight
Pass the stars, the day, the night,
Lord of Angels, on our eyes,
Let eternal morning rise,
And shadows end.

MARY A. LATHBURY

At the last, tenderly,
From the walls of the powerful, fortressed house,
From the clasp of the knitted locks, from the keep of
the well-closed doors,
Let me be wafted.

Let me glide noiselessly forth;
With the key of softness unlock the locks—with a whisper
Set ope the doors, O soul!

Tenderly—be not impatient!
(Strong is your hold, O mortal flesh!
Strong is your hold, O love!)

WALT WHITMAN

The Lord is my light and my salvation—
whom shall I fear?
The Lord is the stronghold of my life—
of whom shall I be afraid?
When evil men advance against me
to devour my flesh,
when my enemies and my foes attack me,
they will stumble and fall.
Though an army besiege me,
my heart will not fear;
though war break out against me,
even then will I be confident.

One thing I ask of the Lord,
this is what I seek:
that I may dwell in the house of the Lord
all the days of my life,
to gaze upon the beauty of the Lord
and to seek Him in His temple.
For in the day of trouble
He will keep me safe in His dwelling;
He will hide me in the shelter of His tabernacle
and set me high upon a rock.

Then my head will be exalted
above the enemies who surround me;
at His tabernacle will I sacrifice with shouts of joy;
I will sing and make music to the Lord.

PSALM 27:1–6

17

Special Prayers

Morning Hymn

O Splendor of God's glory bright,
From light eternal bringeth light,
Thou Light of light, light's living Spring,
True Day, all days illumining.

Come, very Sun of heaven's love,
In lasting radiance from above,
And pour the Holy Spirit's ray
On all we think or do today.

O joyful be the passing day
With thoughts as pure as morning ray,
With faith like noontide shining bright,
Our souls unshadowed by the night.

St. Ambrose

Evening Hymn

Maker of all things! God most high!
Great Ruler of the starry sky!
Robing the day in beauteous light,
In sweet repose the quiet night;
That sleep may our tired limbs restore,
And fit for toil and use once more,
May gently soothe the careworn breast,
and lull our anxious griefs to rest.

St. Ambrose

Cradle Song

Ah Jesus Christ, my Lord most dear,
As Thou wast once an infant here,
So give this little child, I pray,
Thy grace and blessing day by day;
Ah Jesus, Lord Divine,
Guard me this babe of mine!

Now sleep, O sleep, my little child,
Jesus will be thy playmate mild;
Sweet dreams He sendeth thee, I trow,
That full of goodness thou may'st grow;
Ah Jesus, Lord Divine,
Guard me this babe of mine!

So He, who hath all love and might,
Bids thee good morrow and good night.
Blest in His name thou daily art,
My child, thou darling of my heart;
Ah Jesus, Lord Divine,
Guard me this babe of mine!

HENRY OF LAOFENBURG

A Young Person's Prayer

I am young, alas! so young;
And the world has been my foe;

And by hardship, wrong and woe,
Hath my bleeding heart been stung.
There was none, O God! to teach me
What was wrong and what was right.
I have sinned before Thy sight;
Let my cry of anguish reach Thee,
Piercing through the glooms of night,
God of love! . . .

Therefore will I put my trust
In Thy mercy: and I cleave
To that love which can forgive;
To that judgment which is just;
Which can pity all my weakness;
Which hath seen the life-long strife
Of passions fiercer than the knife;
Known the desolating bleakness
Of my desert path through life. . . .

MARY HOWITT

God Speaks . . .

My child, I am the Lord who gives strength in the day of troubles.
Come to Me when it is not well with you.
For the thing that most of all hinders My consolation to you
Is that you are too slow in turning yourself unto prayer.

THOMAS À KEMPIS

My child, it is not necessary to know much to please Me;
it is sufficient to love much. . . .
Are there any for whom thou wouldst pray to Me?
Repeat to Me the names of thy relations, thy friends; after each name
add what thou wouldst have Me do for them.
Ask much, ask much; I love generous souls
who forget themselves for others. . . .
Are there graces thou wouldst ask for thyself?
Write, if thou wilt, a long list of what thou desirest, of all the needs
of thy soul, and come and read it to Me. . . .
Do not hesitate to ask Me for blessings for the body and mind;
for health, memory and success. I can give you all things,
and I always give. . . .
Dost thou dread something painful? Is there in thy heart a vain fear
which is not reasonable, but which is tormenting thee?
Trust thyself wholly to My care. I am here. I see everything.
I will not leave thee. . . .
Well, my child, go now; take up thy work; be silent, humble,
submissive and kind; and come back tomorrow, and bring Me
a heart still more devout and loving.
Tomorrow I shall have more blessings for thee.

Attributed to an Unknown Medieval Saint

I am a Lamp to thee who beholdest Me,
I am a Mirror to thee who perceivest Me,
I am a Door to thee who knockest at Me,
I am a Way to thee a wayfarer.

Jesus Christ

I am the wind which blows over the sea,
I am the wave of the ocean; I am the murmur of the billows,
I am a tear of the Sun, I am the fairest of plants,
I am a wild boar in valour; I am a salmon in the water.
I am a lake in the plain. . . .
I am a word of Science; I am the spearpoint which gives victory;
I am the God which creates in the head of man the fire of
thought.
Who will enlighten each question if not I?

TRADITIONAL CELTIC PRAYER

Be still, and know that I am God.

PSALM 46:10

All shall be well
And all shall be well,
And all manner of things shall be well.

JULIAN OF NORWICH

RESOURCES AND RECOMMENDED READING

Aldrich, Donald Bradshaw, ed. *The Golden Book of Prayer: An Anthology of Prayer.* New York: Permabooks, 1941, 1949.

Anderson, Sherry Ruth, and Patricia Hopkins. *The Feminine Face of God: The Unfolding of the Sacred in Women.* New York: Bantam Books, 1991.

Ashwin, Angela, ed. *The Book of a Thousand Prayers.* New York: Harper-Collins, 1996.

Auger, George, C.S.V. "Prayer, Breath of the Spirit." *Living Prayer* 23.3 (1990): 6–8.

Barrows, Anita, and Joanna Macy, eds. *Rilke's Book of Hours: Love Poems to God.* New York: Riverhead Books, 1996.

Beard, J. R. *Sermons accompanied by Suitable Prayers, Designed to be Used in Families.* Boston: Leonard C. Bowles, 1832.

———. *Meditations on Joy.* New York: DK Publishing, 1995.

———. *Meditations on Love.* New York: DK Publishing, 1995.

———. *Meditations on Peace.* New York: DK Publishing, 1995.

———. *Meditations on Silence.* New York: DK Publishing, 1995.

Beckett, Wendy. *Sister Wendy's Book of Saints.* New York: DK Publishing, 1998.

Bennett, Avis Kimball. "In Relationship with God through Contemplative Prayer." *Living Prayer* 27.1 (1994): 24–26.

Benson, Herbert. *The Relaxation Response.* New York: Morrow, 1975.

Berke, Diane. *The Gentle Smile: Practicing Oneness in Daily Life.* New York: The Crossroad Publishing Company, 1995.

Billy, Dennis J., C.S.S.R. "Re-Imagining God." *Living Prayer* 28.1 (1995): 23–29.

Bloom, Anthony. *Beginning to Pray.* Ramsey, N.J.: Paulist Press, 1970.

Boever, Richard A., C.S.S.R. *Finding God in Everyday Life.* Liguori, Mo.: Liguori Publications, 1988.

Borysenko, Joan. *Minding the Body, Mending the Mind.* New York: Bantam Books, 1988.

Boux, Dorothy. *The Golden Thread: Words of Hope for a Changing World.* London: Shepheard–Walwyn and Bath: Gateway Books, 1990.

Brooke, Avery. *Healing in the Landscape of Prayer.* Cambridge, Mass.: Cowley Publications, 1996.

Brussat, Frederic, and Mary Ann. *Spiritual Literacy: Reading the Sacred in Everyday Life.* New York: Scribner, 1996.

Buechner, Frederick. *The Longing for Home: Recollections and Reflections.* San Francisco: HarperSanFrancisco, 1996.

Burnham, Sophy. *Angel Letters.* New York: Ballantine Books, 1991.

Buttrick, George Arthur. *Prayer.* New York: Abingdon–Cokesbury Press, 1941.

Cassidy, Sheila. *Prayer for Pilgrims: A Book About Prayer for Ordinary People.* New York: The Crossroad Publishing Company, 1980.

Castelli, Jim, ed. *How I Pray: People of Different Religions Share with Us That Most Sacred and Intimate Act of Faith.* New York: Ballantine Books, 1994.

Cleary, William. *Prayers to She Who Is.* New York: The Crossroad Publishing Company, 1995.

Cooper, David A. *Silence, Simplicity, and Solitude: A Guide for Spiritual Retreat.* New York: Bell Tower/Harmony Books, 1992.

——. *Entering the Sacred Mountain: A Mystical Odyssey.* New York: Bell Tower/Harmony Books, 1994.

Cragg, Kenneth, comp. *Alive to God: Muslim and Christian Prayers.* London: Oxford University Press, 1970.

Davis, Avram. *The Way of Flame: A Guide to the Forgotten Mystical Tradition of Jewish Meditation.* San Francisco: HarperSanFrancisco, 1996.

Dillard, Annie. *Pilgrim at Tinker Creek.* New York: Harper's Magazine Press, 1974.

DiNola, Alfonso, comp., Patrick O'Connor, ed., and Rex Benedict, trans. *The Prayers of Man: From Primitive Peoples to Present Times.* London: William Heinemann, Ltd., 1962.

Donnelly, Doris. *Spiritual Fitness: Everyday Exercises for Body and Soul.* San Francisco: HarperSanFrancisco, 1993.

Farrell, Edward. *Prayer Is a Hunger.* Denville, N.J.: Dimension Books, 1972.

Ford–Grabowsky, Mary, ed. *Prayers for All People.* New York: Doubleday, 1995.

Forest, Jim. "Prayer and Sacred Images." *Living Prayer* 28.6 (1995): 10–13.

Gawle, Barbara. *How to Pray: Discovering New Spiritual Growth Through Prayer.* Englewood Cliffs, N.J.: Prentice–Hall, 1984.

Gire, Ken, ed. *Between Heaven and Earth: Prayers and Reflections that Celebrate an Intimate God.* San Francisco: HarperSanFrancisco, 1997.

Greene, Barbara, and Victor Gollancz. *A God of a Hundred Names.* New York: Doubleday, 1962.

Griffin, Emilie. *Wilderness Time: A Guide for Spiritual Retreat.* San Francisco: HarperSanFrancisco, 1997.

Groeschel, Benedict J., O.F.M. *Listening at Prayer.* Ramsey, N.J.: Paulist Press, 1984.

Hanh, Thich Nhat. *The Miracle of Mindfulness: A Manual of Meditation.* Boston: Beacon Press, 1975, 1976.

———. *Living Buddha, Living Christ.* New York: Riverhead Books, 1995.

———. *Cultivating the Mind of Love: The Practice of Looking Deeply in the Mahayana Buddhist Tradition.* Berkeley, Calif.: Parallax Press, 1996.

Johnston, William. *The Inner Eye of Love: Mysticism and Religion.* San Francisco: Harper & Row Publishers, 1978.

Kabat–Zinn, Jon. *Full Catastrophe Living: Using the Wisdom of Your Body and Mind to Face Stress, Pain, and Illness.* New York: Delacorte Press, 1990.

Kaisch, Ken. *Finding God: A Handbook of Christian Meditation.* Mahwah, N.J.: Paulist Press, 1994.

Kieling, Jared T., ed. *The Gift of Prayer: A Treasury of Personal Prayer from the World's Spiritual Traditions.* New York: The Continuum Publishing Company, 1995.

Kornfield, Jack, and Christina Feldman. *Soul Food: Stories to Nourish the Spirit and the Heart.* San Francisco: HarperSanFrancisco, 1991, 1996.

L'Engle, Madeleine, with Carole F. Chase. *Glimpses of Grace: Daily Thoughts and Reflections.* San Francisco: HarperSanFrancisco, 1996.

Martin, Francis. *Touching God.* Denville, N.J.: Dimension Books, 1975.

Merrill, Nan C. *Psalms For Praying: An Invitation to Wholeness.* New York: The Continuum Publishing Company, 1996.

Merton, Thomas. *New Seeds of Contemplation.* New York: New Directions Books, 1972; The Abbey of Gethsemani, Inc., 1961.

Middleton, John. "Praying Our Prayers of Yearning." *Living Prayer* 28.6 (1995): 7–9.

Murray, Andrew. *The Ministry of Intercessory Prayer.* Minneapolis: Bethany House Publishers, 1981.

Muto, Susan. *Pathways of Spiritual Living.* Petersham, Mass.: St. Bede's Publications, 1984.

Muto, Susan, and Adrian van Kaam. *Practicing the Prayer of Presence.* Mineola, N.Y.: Resurrection Press, 1993.

Newman, John Henry, ed., trans. *The Devotions of Bishop Andrewes.* New York: George H. Richmond & Co., 1987.

Ninde, Edward S. *Nineteen Centuries of Christian Song*. New York: Fleming H. Rowell Company, 1938.

Norris, Kathleen. *Amazing Grace: A Vocabulary of Faith*. New York: Riverhead Books, 1998.

Nouwen, Henri J. M. *The Way of the Heart*. New York: Ballantine Books, 1981.

Occhiogrosso, Peter. *Through the Labyrinth: Stories of the Search for Spiritual Transformation in Everyday Life*. New York: Viking Penguin, 1991.

——. *The Joy of Sects: A Spirited Guide to the World's Religious Traditions*. New York: Doubleday, 1994.

Panati, Charles. *Sacred Origin of Profound Things: The Stories Behind the Rites and Rituals of the World's Religions*. New York: Penguin Arkana, 1996.

Pennington, Basil, O.C.S.O. *Centering Prayer: Renewing an Ancient Christian Prayer Form*. New York: Doubleday/Image Books, 1980.

Radha, Swami Sivananda. *Mantras: Words of Power*. Spokane, Wash.: Timeless Books, 1994.

Raghavan, V., trans. *Prayers, Praises and Psalms: Selections from The Vedas, Upanishads, Epics, Gita, Puranas, Agamas, Tantras, Kavyas and the Writings of the Acharyas and Others*. Foreword by Mahatma Gandhi. Madras, India: G. A. Natesan & Co., 1948.

Roberts, Elizabeth, and Elias Amidon, eds. *Earth Prayers from Around the World: 365 Prayers, Poems and Invocations for Honoring the Earth*. San Francisco: HarperSanFrancisco, 1991.

——. *Life Prayers from Around the World: 365 Prayers, Blessings and Affirmations to Celebrate the Human Journey*. San Francisco: HarperSanFrancisco, 1996.

Roth, Nancy. *A New Christian Yoga*. Cambridge, Mass.: Cowley Publications, 1989.

——. *The Breath of God: An Approach to Prayer*. Cambridge, Mass.: Cowley Publications, 1990.

——. *Organic Prayer: Cultivating Your Relationship with God*. Cambridge, Mass.: Cowley Publications, 1993.

Ryan, Thomas, C.S.P. *Prayer of Heart and Body: Meditation and Yoga as Christian Spiritual Practice*. Mahwah, N.J.: Paulist Press, 1995.

Ruffing, Janet K., R.S.M. "As Refined By Fire." *Living Prayer* 28.2 (1995): 3–7.

Salwak, Dale, ed. *The Wisdom of Judaism*. Novato, Calif.: New World Library, 1997.

Schroeder, Celeste Snowber. *In the Womb of God: Creative Nurturing for the Soul*. Liguori, Mo.: Triumph Books, 1995.

Sergio, Lisa, ed. *Prayers of Women*. New York: Harper & Row, Publishers, 1965.

Shannon, William H. *Silence on Fire: The Prayer of Awareness*. New York: The Crossroad Publishing Company, 1991.

Simpkins, C. Alexander, and Annellen M. Simpkins. *Principles of Meditation: Eastern Wisdom for the Western Mind*. Boston: Charles E. Tuttle Company, 1996.

Slesin, S., and E. Gwathmey, eds. *Amen: Prayers and Blessings from Around the World*. New York: Penguin Books, 1995.

Smith, Delia. *A Journey into God*. San Francisco: Harper & Row Publishers, 1988.

Smith, Huston. *The World's Religions: A Completely Revised and Updated Edition of the Religions of Man*. San Francisco: HarperSanFrancisco, 1991.

Snow, Kimberley. *Keys to the Open Gate: A Woman's Spirituality Sourcebook*. Berkeley, Calif.: Conari Press, 1994.

Studdert-Kennedy, G. A. *The Wicket Gate or Plain Bread*. New York: Richard R. Smith, Inc. 1923.

Sutter, John Wallace. *Prayers for a New World*. New York: Scribner, 1964.

Van de Weyer, Robert, ed. *The HarperCollins Book of Prayer: A Treasury of Prayer Through the Ages*. San Francisco: HarperSanFrancisco, 1993.

Whiston, Charles. *Pray: A Study of Distinctive Christian Praying*. Grand Rapids, Mich.: Wm. B. Eerdmans Publishing Company, 1972.

Wiederkehr, Macrina. *The Song of the Seed: A Monastic Way of Tending the Soul*. San Francisco: HarperSanFrancisco, 1995.

Zaehner, R. C., ed. *The Concise Encyclopedia of Living Faiths*. Boston: Beacon Press, 1959.

Zaleski, Philip. *The Recollected Heart*. San Francisco: HarperSanFrancisco, 1995.

Zuercher, Suzanne, O.S.B. "Have You Tried One of These Mantras?" *Living Prayer* 28.5 (1995): 3–6.

About the Authors

Joseph Nassal, C.P.P.S., spent three years as the director of Shantivanam, a contemplative house of prayer in Kansas City, Kansas. Shantivanam (meaning "Forest of Peace" in Sanskrit) is a nonsectarian community of committed lay people devoted to the ministry of prayer. The community was founded by Reverend Nassal's predecessor and mentor, Reverend Edward Hayes, the author of numerous classics such as *Pray All Ways, Prayers for a Planetary Pilgrim* and *Secular Sanctity*.

Reverend Nassal is a writer, editor and contributor to numerous periodicals. He has been involved in retreat and renewal ministry for over a decade and currently travels nationwide to lead retreats on the topic of prayer. His recent seminars—which are so popular that he's booked a year in advance—focus on the theme of moving from meditation to prayer.

Coauthor **Nancy Burke** has written two books for Random House, *Meditations for Health* and *Teachers Are Special*, and has cowritten a number of other books including *St. John's Wort: The Miracle Medicine, The American Association of Oriental Medicine's Complete Guide to Chinese Herbal Medicine* and *Active Wellness: A Personalized 10-Step Plan for Health Empowerment* for various publishers. She contributes to several spirituality and New Age magazines, including *New Age Journal*, and is the former media editor of *BodyMindSpirit* magazine. Her writing has been excerpted for books, magazines and television. She lives with her daughter in New England.